Global Humanities
Studies in Histories, Cultures, and Societies

02/2015
Religion and Poverty

Global Humanities
Studies in Histories, Cultures, and Societies

02/2015

Religion and Poverty

Edited by Frank Jacob

Neofelis Verlag

Global Humanities – Studies in Histories, Cultures, and Societies
02/2015: Religion and Poverty
Ed. by Frank Jacob

German National Library Cataloguing in Publication Data
A catalogue record for this book is available from the German National Library: http://dnb.d-nb.de

Cover Design: Marija Skara
Printed by PRESSEL Digitaler Produktionsdruck, Remshalden
Printed on FSC-certified paper.
ISSN: 2199-3939
ISBN (Print): 978-3-95808-004-1
ISBN (PDF): 978-3-943414-94-3

Global Humanities appears biannually.

Contents

Artistic Perspective

Editorial

> Religious suffering is, at one and the same time, the expression of real suffering and a protest against real suffering. Religion is the sigh of the oppressed creature, the heart of a heartless world, and the soul of soulless conditions. It is the opium of the people.[1]

Karl Marx (1818–1883) is known for his "repeated, and often polemical, statements against religion"[2] through which he became an important predecessor of many of the radical critics of religion in the 20th century, including Georges Bataille (1897–1962), Rudolf Bultmann (1884–1976), Gustavo Gutiérrez (*1928), and Martin Heidegger (1889–1976).[3] However, the opium referred to in his oft-quoted statement (given above) can be read as occupying an ambivalent conceptual position. Here, Opium (or religion) might not only be interpreted as a "destructive narcotic", but "also a protest" against the real suffering of the people.[4] Opium held something of a double meaning during the late 19th century: as both a useful and inexpensive medicine, and also as a source of illness and destructive addiction. In this way, Opium also existed as a "multidimensional metaphor"[5] for Marx.

Through their numerous writings on religion,[6] Marx and Friedrich Engels (1820–1895) formulated the widely known argument that religion can only be explained through an exploration of the social and economic factors responsible for its condition.[7] Despite the fact that Marx argued for an abolition of religion, he also recognized that religion appeared to offer a form of

1 Karl Marx: Contribution to the Critique of Hegel's Philosophy of Law: Introduction. In: *Marx and Engels Collected Works*, vol. 3. Moscow: Progress 1975, pp. 175–187, here p. 175.

2 James Luchte: Marx and the Sacred. In: *Journal of Church and State* 51,3 (2009), pp. 413–437, here p. 413.

3 Ibid., pp. 414–415.

4 Roland Boer: Opium, Idols and Revolution: Marx and Engels on Religion. In: *Religion Compass* 5,11 (2011), pp. 698–707, here p. 703.

5 Ibid.

6 Friedrich Engels / Karl Marx: *Die heilige Familie, oder, Kritik der kritischen Kritik, gegen Bruno Bauer & Consorten.* Frankfurt am Main: Rütten 1845; Karl Marx: Contribution to the Critique of Hegel's Philosophy of Law, trans. from German by Martin Milligan / Barbara Ruhemann. In: *Marx and Engels Collected Works*, vol. 3. London: Lawrence & Wishart 1975, pp. 3–129; Karl Marx: *Ökonomisch-philosophische Manuskripte. Geschrieben von April bis Aug. 1844. Karl Marx. Nach der Handschrift.* Leipzig: Reclam 1968.

7 Boer: Opium, p. 699. For a detailed study on Marx's and Engels' criticism of religion, see Roland Boer: *Criticism of Earth: On Marx, Engels and Theology*. Leiden: Brill 2012.

liberation, rather than oppression, to those who suffered in poverty.[8] As such, religion might become an expression of protest for those who suffered; an appropriate reply to the hardships of human life. Consequently Marx arrived at the formulation that religion was "the wrong way of protesting something that deserves to be protested."[9]

Whether or not one sits in agreement with Marx's criticisms, religion was and remains a significant part of human culture and belief systems, both now and throughout history. Religion not only bears a relationship to poverty, but as Lisa A. Keister has argued, it is "a very strong predictor of adult wealth"[10]. In this way, we can also trace a general interrelationship between wealth and religion. Further, the "success of capitalism and the democratization of higher education did not diminish religious life"[11], a fact that would appear to undermine Marx's claim that religion was merely an expression of and mechanism for control of those suffering in poverty. However, we cannot neglect the current reality of the apparently strong religious beliefs in regions of the world that are suffering from poverty – the so called "Third World" – and a concomitant, general decline of religious beliefs and traditions in many parts of the industrialized world. Poverty, in addition to other factors such as race,[12] remains a distinguishing force for religion.

We can describe a three-pronged relationship between religion and poverty, wherein religion:

1) redirects the thoughts of the poor to religious concerns;

2) provides the necessary moral structures for a culture and society that might stimulate generosity;

3) encourages attempts to alleviate poverty itself.[13]

8 Kathryn Lofton: The Sigh of the Oppressed? Marxism and Religion in America Today. In: *New Labour Forum* 21,3 (2012), pp. 58–65, here pp. 58–59.

9 Ibid., p. 59. Antonio Gramsci (1891–1937) also suggested that religion could be seen as a form of protest against a hegemonial system. See Dwight B. Billings: Religion as Opposition: A Gramscian Analysis. In: *American Journal of Sociology* 96,1 (1990), pp. 1–31, here pp. 6–9.

10 Lisa A. Keister: *Faith and Money: How Religion Contributes to Wealth and Poverty*. New York: Cambridge UP 2011, p. 132.

11 Lofton: The Sigh, p. 58.

12 Matthew O. Hunt: Religion, Race / Ethnicity, and Beliefs about Poverty. In: *Social Science Quarterly* 83,3 (2002), pp. 810–831, here pp. 815–816.

13 Jaco Beyers: The Effect of Religion on Poverty. In: *HTS Teologiese Studies / Theological Studies* 70,1 (2014), Art. #2614, 8 pages. http://dx.doi.org/10.4102/hts.v70i1.2614 (accessed 01.06.2015), p. 1.

The effects of this relationship, however, can be read as either positive or negative. Poverty itself appears to have no tangibly positive effect on humanity, despite the claims of certain religious figures whose personal catharsis emerged through poverty.[14]

Most notably in Latin America, the positive effect of religion – namely a possible alleviation of poverty – was underscored by a reinterpretation of Christian theology during the 1960s, the so-called ‚liberation theology' as formulated by Gutiérrez and Juan Luis Segundo (1925–1996). Their intention was simple: "to transform society through social action and on the basis of the Christian message of justice, peace, and love."[15] Religion consequently was no longer seen as an offer for theodicies[16], but as a feasible solution for the abolishment of poverty. However, both religion and poverty are still in existence, and both seem to be resistant to disappearance. Consequently, neither Marxist theories nor philanthropic attempts to solve global poverty could be read as offering successful or suitable answers to the problem of poverty. It is far more likely that religion and poverty are inseparable elements of human history, a point that this present volume attempts to address, by probing some of the questions implicated in this specific interrelation.

The first contribution by Benjamin Beit-Hallahmi provides a survey of sociological discussions about the interrelationship between religion and poverty, focusing on the parameters of crisis, sectarianism, race, and mobility as offering possible explanations for human religiosity. The following two articles by Sabine Müller and Divya Kannan focus on historical perspectives concerning the interrelationship of religion and poverty. While Müller's article analyzes Lucian's *Alexander of Abonuteichos*' historic assessment of poverty and religion, Kannan's contribution highlights the relationship between poverty and the education program of the London Missionary Society in South India during the 19th century.

Following the sociological and historical perspectives, the next section focuses on religious perspectives. Alvin Lim analyzes the role of an excessively "performed" poverty within the Daoist practice of money-burning in Singapore, a performance through which believers hope to gain salvation. Jeremiah Unterman then provides a close reading of the Jewish Bible to gain an insight

14 Francis of Assisi (1181/1182–1226) would be one example.

15 Judith Soares: Religion and Poverty in the Caribbean. In: *Peace Review: A Journal of Social Justice* 20,2 (2008), pp. 226–234, here p. 226.

16 Max Weber: *Economy and Society*, vol. 1. Totawa, NJ: Bedminster 1921, pp. 495–498.

into the social and ethical aspects of its descriptions and rules. The section on religious perspectives concludes with the contribution by Logan Cochrane and Waleed Chellan, whose article is dealing with the interrelationship of religious adherence and economic status in the modern Muslim world.
The final article by Atara Moscovich adds an artistic perspective to the reading of the interrelationship between religion and poverty. By giving a detailed interpretation of Giovanni Bellini's (ca. 1430–1516) *Sacred Allegory*, Moscovich explores how artistic interpretations of the interrelationship of religion and poverty were expressed in the religious art of the Renaissance.
The second volume of *Global Humanities* again brings together researchers from different disciplines, in order to discuss what presents itself as a driving question within the humanities from a global and interdisciplinary perspective. This volume was made possible through the professionalism of its contributors, to whom I extend my thanks. I would also like to express my gratitude to Matthias Naumann and Frank Schlöffel from Neofelis Press for their invaluable and steady support.

Frank Jacob
New York, June 2015

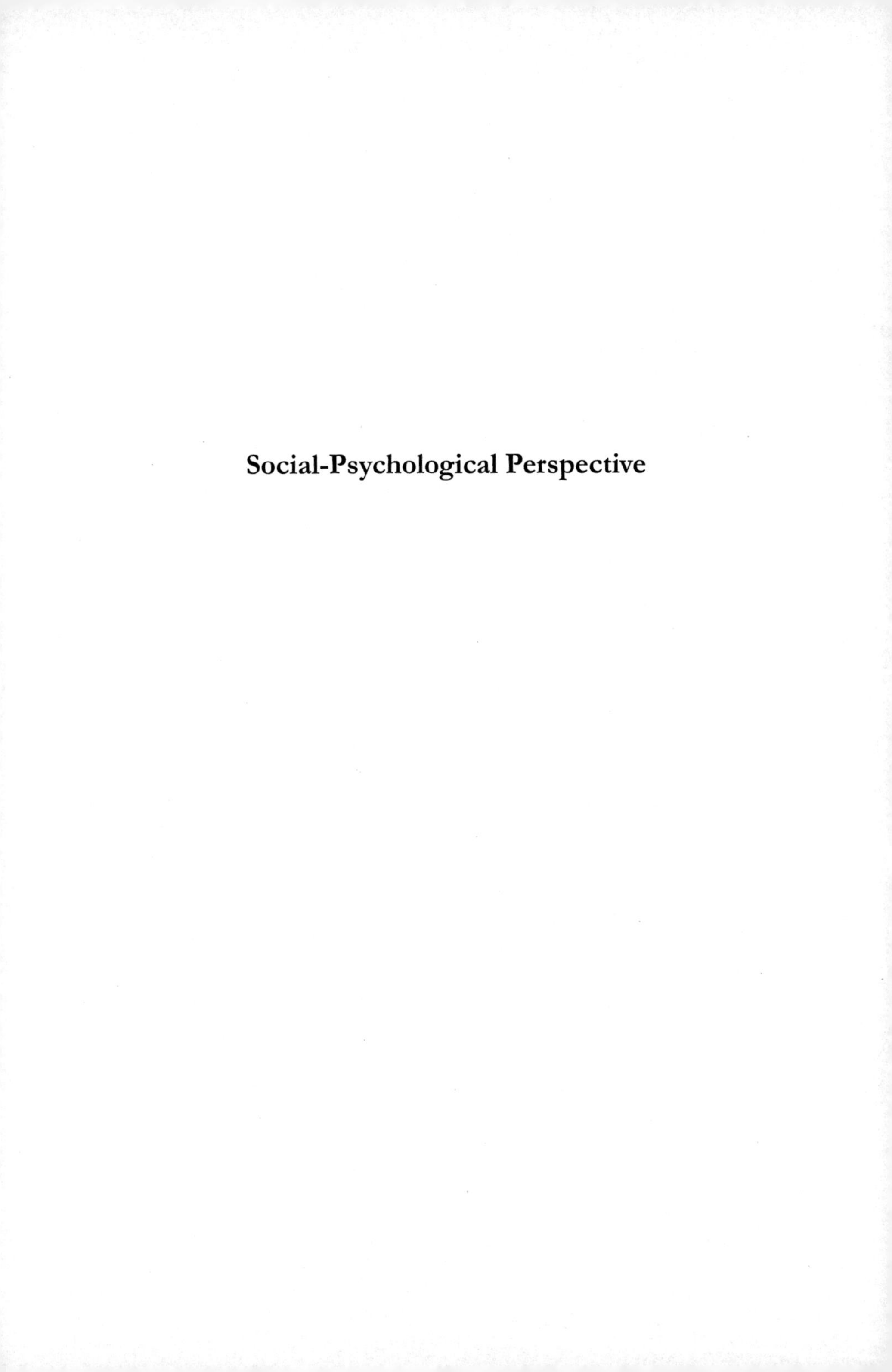

Social-Psychological Perspective

Deprivation and Religiosity

Between Cargo Cults and Existential Anxiety

Benjamin Beit-Hallahmi

Secular explanations of religion are based on the notion of deprivation, as they all assume the presence of unmet needs. The most common explanations for serious religious involvement in both individuals and collectivities, found in the writings of historians, sociologists, anthropologists, political science scholars, or psychologists, use the terms deprivation, frustration, suffering, crisis, vulnerability, or insecurity. Some may feel uneasy with this choice of terms, and regard it as alienated, sanitized, too psychological, or euphemistic. They may feel that suffering, hunger, and violence should be uncovered and confronted without the use of an academic vocabulary. To judge the vision behind the large body of literature involved, we should read carefully, with eyes open for the researchers' stance beyond academic conventions.

Deprivation explanations lead to the prediction that with lower levels of suffering, religiosity would decline in both individuals and groups. This article reviews hypotheses and empirical surveys on religiosity and poverty, with an emphasis on the literature in the humanities and social sciences over the past 100 years, which is when most research has been carried out.

It should be noted that social science explanations of most human behaviors, both individual and social, are based on deprivation or deficiency. The terminology of strain, crisis, deficiency, and dislocation is used in history and the social sciences not only to explain religion, but to explain secular ideologies and secular political movements.[1]

The best known formulation linking religious activity to both material and psychological deprivation was offered by Karl Marx: "Religious suffering is at the same time an expression of real suffering and a protest against real suffering. Religion is the sigh of the oppressed creature, the heart of a heartless world, and the soul of soulless conditions. It is the opium of the people."[2] A century later, a similar view was offered by the sociologist Kingsley Davis:

1 Benjamin Beit-Hallahmi: *Despair and Deliverance: Private Salvation in Contemporary Israel.* Albany, NY: SUNY 1992; Neil J. Smelser: *Theory of Collective Behaviour.* London: Routledge & Kegan Paul 1962.

2 Karl Marx: *Early Writings.* New York: McGraw-Hill 1964, pp. 43–44.

"The greater his [man's] disappointment in this life, the greater his faith in the next. Thus, the existence of goals beyond this world serves to compensate people for frustrations they inevitably experience in striving to reach socially acquired and socially valuable ends."[3] An inverse relationship is predicted between readiness and opportunity for instrumental coping on the one hand, and involvement in religion on the other.[4] According to Charles Glock, religious activities "are likely to compensate for feelings of deprivation rather than to eliminate its causes."[5]

Marx described the projective product in religion as an "inverse world", in which fantasy compensates for real suffering.[6] In agreement, the sociologists Rodney Stark and William S. Bainbridge[7] described religion as providing "supernatural general compensators", imaginary rewards when real rewards are unavailable. It seems that there are indeed two opposite types of response to economic and social deprivation: an other-worldly fantasy response, and an instrumental action response.

Religious believers are expected to obey cosmic forces and be rewarded by feelings of vicarious participation in the power and wisdom of those forces. The feeling of social superiority and 'chosenness', provided by religious groups, must be viewed as a compensation for actual frustrations. The underprivileged may consider themselves members of some spiritual elite,[8] which reduces the potential for political action, either by turning them away from social action, or by adjusting to the system.

The scholarly literature offers thousands of case studies which illustrate the connection between psychological or material deficiencies and increasing religiosity. Unmet needs are viewed by historians or sociologists as causing both the appearance of new religious movements and the readiness of some individuals to join such movements. Religious movements emerge because of

3 Kingsley Davis: *Human Society*. New York: Macmillan 1948, p. 532.

4 Benjamin Beit-Hallahmi: *Prolegomena to the Psychological Study of Religion*. Lewisburg, PA: Bucknell UP 1989.

5 Charles Glock: The Role of Deprivation in the Origin and Evolution of Religious Groups. In: Robert Lee / Martin E. Marty (eds): *Religion and Social Conflict*. New York: Oxford UP 1964, pp. 24–36, here p. 29.

6 Karl Marx / Friedrich Engels: *K. Marx and F. Engels on Religion*. Moscow: Foreign Languages Publishing 1957.

7 Rodney Stark / William S. Bainbridge: *A Theory of Religion*. New York: Lang 1987.

8 Werner Stark: *The Sociology of Religion*, vol. 2: Sectarian Religion. London: Routledge 1967, p. 702.

> stresses and tensions differentially experienced within the total society. Change in the economic position of a particular group [...]industrialization and urbanization [...] Particular groups are rendered marginal by some process of social change; there is a sudden need for a new interpretation of their social position or for a trans-valuation of their experience.[9]

In describing one Japanese new religious movement, Hideo Hashimoto and William McPherson stated that "[i]n both the United States and Japan, membership data suggest that members of the Sokagakkai are marginal in social and economic characteristics."[10]

Under particular circumstances, changing religious affiliation may be an attempt to cope with deprivation whose source is religious identity. Thus, groups of Dalit ("untouchables") in India have converted to Islam, Christianity, or Buddhism, trying (with limited success) to shake off the stigma created by the Hindu caste system.[11] Some conversion movements to Protestantism (originating in North America) among native tribes in South America reflect a desire to adjust to the market economy and become "modern".[12]

Multiple deprivations (e.g. being of an ethnic minority, with low income, and less education) would make religious involvement more likely. All over the world, religious individuals are more likely to be female, over the age of 50, and of a lower social class.[13] Thomas C. Campbell and Yoshio Fukuyama[14] defined social deprivation on the basis of age, sex, education, socio-economic status, and place of residence (rural or urban). Using this combined index, they found that traditional beliefs were stronger among older people, females, less educated people, the poor, and the rural. In a study of American Roman

9 Bryan R. Wilson: *Patterns of Sectarianism*. London: Heinemann 1967, p. 31.

10 Hideo Hashimoto / William McPherson: Rise and Decline of Sokagakkai Japan and the United States. In: *Review of Religious Research* 17 (1976), pp. 82–92, here p. 83.

11 Adele M. Fiske: Religion and Buddhism among India's New Buddhists. In: *Social Research* 36 (1969), pp. 123–137; Arvar Bopegamage: Status Seekers in India: A Sociological Study of the Neo-Buddhist Movement. In: *European Journal of Sociology / Archives Européennes de Sociologie* 20 (1979), pp. 19–39.

12 Conrad L. Kanagy: The Formation and Development of a Protestant Conversion Movement among the Highland Quichua of Ecuador. In: *Sociological Analysis* 51 (1990), pp. 205–217; Ted C. Lewellen: Deviant Religion and Cultural Evolution: The Aymara Case. In: *Journal for the Scientific Study of Religion* 18 (1979), pp. 243–251.

13 Benjamin Beit-Hallahmi / Michael Argyle: *The Psychology of Religious Behavior, Belief and Experience*. London: Routledge 1997; Benjamin Beit-Hallahmi: *Psychological Perspectives on Religion and Religiosity*. London / New York: Routledge 2014; James Davison Hunter: *American Evangelicalism: Conservative Religion and the Quandary of Modernity*. New Brunswick: Rutgers UP 1983.

14 Thomas C. Campbell / Yoshio Fukuyama: *The Fragmented Layman*. Philadelphia: Pilgrim 1970.

Catholics, Stefan Christopher et al.[15] used a similar combined index of social deprivation, including sex, age and education, which positively correlated with several measures of religiosity.

Glock, Benjamin B. Ringer, and Earl R. Babbie[16] found that individuals who were older, female, unmarried, having lower income or less education were more likely to be religiously involved. Consumers of religious services through the electronic media in the Southern United States were more likely to be older, female, poor, and with less education.[17] James Davison Hunter[18] found that support for Christian doctrinal orthodoxy in the United States was highest among women and retired men, with low education and income, living in rural areas of the South and Midwest.

Deprivation is also related to rare and unusual forms of religious involvement. Witch killing, which seems incomprehensible, is a scapegoating ritual in reaction to material want. The article of Edward Miguel[19] demonstrated that the frequency of witch killing, but not of other murders, rises with the incidence of extreme rainfall, which threatens agriculture and community survival. Similarly, possession phenomena in many cultures have been interpreted as expressions of discontent by deprived groups.[20]

Crisis Religions

Millenarian movements, offering dreams of a new cosmic order, are likely to be born under conditions of social upheaval:

> Following a disaster such as an epidemic, famine, revolution or war, people feel vulnerable, confused and full of anxiety, and they turn to millennial beliefs in order to account for the otherwise meaningless events. The disaster is given meaning as a prelude to the messianic period so that the deepest despair gives way to the greatest hope.[21]

15 Stefan Christopher / John Fearon / John McCoy / Charles Nobbe: Social Deprivation and Religiosity. In: *Journal for the Scientific Study of Religion* 10 (1971), pp. 385–393.

16 Charles Y. Glock / Benjamin B. Ringer / Earl R. Babbie: *To Comfort and to Challenge.* Berkeley: University of California Press 1967.

17 William Stacey / Anson Shupe: Correlates of Support for the Electronic Church. In: *Journal for the Scientific Study of Religion* 21 (1982), pp. 291–303.

18 Hunter: *American Evangelicalism*, p. 130.

19 Edward Miguel: Poverty and Witch Killing. In: *Review of Economic Studies* 72 (2005), pp. 1153–1172.

20 Ioan M. Lewis: Spirit Possession and Deprivation Cults. In *Man* 1 (1966), pp. 307–329.

21 Steven Sharot: Jewish Millenarianism: A Comparison of Medieval Communities. In: *Comparative Studies in Society and History* 22 (1980), pp. 394–415, here p. 401.

Hugh Trevor-Roper described

> that stock refuge of the oppressed: mysticism, the Messiah, the Millennium. As the defeated humanists of Spain sank into private ecstasies […] as the Anabaptists of the seventeenth century manipulated their Scriptural logarithms to hasten the Apocalypse, so also the Jews of the Dispersion deviated into mystical heresies, counted the days to the Millennium, or discovered the Messiah.[22]

Historians tie the appearance of religious fervor to preceding material hardships involving a major loss of life: "It is significant that at the time of the First Crusade of 1095 the areas which were swept by mass enthusiasm had for ten years been afflicted by famine and drought and for five years by plague, while the crusades of 1146, 1309, and 1320 were all precluded by famines".[23]

Examples of millennial movements which followed social dislocations, catastrophes, plagues, famines, and massacres, are provided by Sylvia Thrupp,[24] Norman Cohn,[25] and Michael Barkun.[26] Robert Wuthnow, after reviewing the histories of revitalization movements, from Anabaptists in Europe in the 16th century to "Cargo cults" in 20th century Melanesia,[27] concluded that they were all responses to the destruction of traditional social and economic patterns, and that they "provide hopes that transcend immediate deprivations"[28].

The voodoo religion of Haiti flourishes under the conditions of the worst possible deprivation, in one of the world's poorest countries, where individuals are doomed to a life without any relief from the need to just survive.[29] The African movement known as Bwiti has been interpreted by researchers[30] as a reaction to malaise and frustration under colonialism. Referring to the Navaho Peyote movement, Mary Douglas describes

22 Hugh Trevor-Roper: *Historical Essays*. London: Macmillan 1963, pp. 148–149.

23 Norman Cohn: Medieval Millenarianism: Its Bearings on the Comparative Study of Millenarian Movements. In: Sylvia Thrupp (ed.): *Millennial Dreams in Action*. The Hague: Mouton 1962, pp. 31–43, here p. 34.

24 Thrupp (ed.): *Millennial Dreams in Action*.

25 Norman Cohn: *The Pursuit of the Millennium*. London: Secker & Warburg 1957.

26 Michael Barkun: *Disaster and the Millennium*. New Haven: Yale UP 1974.

27 Glynn Cochrane: *Big Men and Cargo Cults*. Oxford: Clarendon 1970, p. 62.

28 Robert Wuthnow: World Order and Religious Movements. In: Albert Bergesen (ed.): *Studies of the Modern World-System*. New York: Academic Press 1980, pp. 57–75.

29 On Voodoo in Haiti, see Maya Deren: *Divine Horsemen: The Living Gods of Haiti*. London: Thames & Hudson 1953.

30 James W. Fernandez: *Bwiti: An Ethnography of the Religious Imagination in Africa*. Princeton: Princeton UP 1982.

> the new Navaho, impoverished [...] inadequately involved in the [...] economy [...] could not count on his kinsmen. He was alone. Eating peyote gave him a sense of greatly enhanced personal worth and a sense of direct communion with the supernatural. Notice that his God has become like himself.[31]

The Chinese Taiping movement in the mid–nineteenth century led to a major civil war, where possibly 20 million were killed. Its leader claimed to be the son of the Christian God and the brother of the mythological Jesus. He also attacked the feudal regime and laid out a plan for a modernized China. The movement mobilized the poor masses into a force that became a real threat to the ruling Manchu dynasty. The rulers would have been defeated without the intervention of Britain and the United States on their side.[32]

The Ghost Dance, a rebellion by Native Americans against White settlers, started as a totally non–violent apocalyptic dream. It represented a traditional response to externally imposed oppression and deprivation. Its doctrine was based on ideas about the coming triumph of the natives over the Europeans, material prosperity at the expense of Europeans, the resurrection of the dead, and the return to pre-colonial bliss, including the reappearance of buffalo herds. The eventual outcome would be a renewal of native existence, forever free of death, disease, and misery. To bring this about, natives had to perform the sacred dance. Believers were also exhorted to discard all warlike behaviors.[33]

The largest wave of the Ghost Dance movement rose in 1890 in the western United States, when 45 North American tribes, inspired by the prophet Wovoka, were involved. Michael P. Carroll[34] showed that the recent extermination of the buffalo led particular Native American tribes to join the Ghost Dance of 1890, and resulting population decline was another factor.[35]

Wovoka presented himself as the messenger of a messianic kingdom, soon to be established under Jesus Christ. In Wovoka's visions, the native dead

31 Mary Douglas: *Natural Symbols: Explorations in Cosmology*. London: Barrie & Jenkins 1973, p. 33.

32 Stephen R. Platt: *Autumn in the Heavenly Kingdom: China, the West, and the Epic Story of the Taiping Civil War*. New York: Knopf 2012.

33 Weston La Barre: *The Ghost Dance: The Origins of Religion*. New York: Doubleday 1970; Vittorio Lanternari: *The Religions of the Oppressed. A Study of Modern Messianic Cults*. New York: Knopf 1963; James Mooney: *The Ghost Dance Religion and the Sioux Outbreak of 1890*. Chicago: University of Chicago Press 1965.

34 Michael P. Carroll: Revitalization Movements and Social Structure: Some Quantitative Tests. In: *American Sociological Review* 40 (1975), pp. 389–401.

35 Russell Thornton: *We Shall Live Again; The 1870 and 1890 Ghost Dance Movements as Demographic Revitalization*. Cambridge: Cambridge UP 1986.

would appear around God's throne, the natives would recover their lands and their lost way of life, while the Whites would disappear. The Ghost Dance itself was designed to secure communication with the dead and hasten the coming of the messianic age. Men and women, dressed in white, danced in circles, singing "revealed" songs and reaching ecstasy. Wovoka's followers also believed that they were immune to bullets. The Ghost Dance of 1890 ended with the massacre at Wounded Knee, South Dakota, on December 29, 1890, in which chief Sitting Bull and between 150 and 300 Sioux were killed. Wovoka survived the Ghost Dance, died in 1932, and is buried, under the name Jack Wilson, in western Nevada.

The Ghost Dance has been compared to Cargo cults, a collective term for a variety of nativist movements which have appeared most often in Oceania, and promoted the belief in obtaining "cargo," i. e. manufactured goods and wealth, through purely religious means. Sometimes ancestors are expected to return, delivering the cargo. In all of these cases, as we judge them today, we regard the natives as victims of European colonization and recognize their deprivation and oppression. We should recall that earlier generations saw them as savages committing acts of terrorism.

Sectarianism in Modern Society

Sectarian movements are the crisis religions of the First World. Since the early twentieth century, sociologists have proposed a distinction between sect and church, and between sect-religiosity and church-religiosity. As opposed to the church-type organization, characterized by an adaptive stance towards society around it, birth-based membership, and universalism, sect-type groups are characterized by high commitment, a converted membership, and separatism towards the larger society.[36]

Research shows that

> sects tend to attract individuals with limited secular opportunities [...] classes of people experiencing relatively limited secular opportunities (such as minorities, women, and the young) are more likely than others to choose sect membership over mainline church membership [...] a general decline in secular opportunities, such as that which occurs during recessions, will make sectarian groups more attractive.[37]

36 Beit-Hallahmi: *Psychological Perspectives on Religion and Religiosity*, the book; id. / Michael Argyle: *The Psychology of Religious Behavior, Belief and Experience*; Bryan R. Wilson: *Sects and Society*. London: Heinemann 1961.

37 Lawrence Iannaccone: Why Strict Churches are Strong. In: *American Journal of Sociology* 99 (1994), pp. 1180–1211, here p. 1201.

The lower-class and minority group origins of sect-type movements in the United States[38] and elsewhere[39] have been well documented. John L. Gillin[40] described sects as protest groups of the poor in the USA. Berton H. Kaplan[41] described sect-type religiosity among the lower-class in the US as "religious escapism".[42]

John D. Photiadis and William Schweiker[43] showed that powerlessness was related to joining authoritarian organizations and sectarian movements, and suggested that in a period of fast social change membership in authoritarian groups will rise. Stephen M. Sales[44] found that authoritarian churches become more attractive in times of insecurity, such as the great depression of the 1930s in the United States. During four periods of heightened economic insecurity in the twentieth century, Americans have been found to be more likely to attend churches that strictly adhered to doctrine.[45]

38 Michael Barkun: *Crucible of the Millennium: The Burned-over District of New York in the 1840s.* Syracuse: Syracuse UP 1986; Anton T. Boisen: Economic Distress and Religious Experience: A Study of the Holy Rollers. In: *Psychiatry* 2 (1939), pp. 185–94; Anton T. Boisen: *Religion in Crisis and Custom.* New York: Harper 1955; Nathan L. Gerrard: The Serpent-Handling Religions of West Virginia. In: *Trans-Action* 5 (1968), pp. 22–28; Nathan L. Gerrard: Churches of the Stationary Poor in Southern Appalachia. In: John Photiadis / Harry Schwarzweller (eds): *Change in Rural Appalachia.* Philadelphia: University of Pennsylvania Press 1970, pp. 99–114; John B. Holt: Holiness Religion: Cultural Shock and Social Reorganization. In: *American Sociological Review* 5 (1940), pp. 740–747; Thomas F. Hoult: *The Sociology of Religion.* New York: Holt 1958; Milton Yinger: *Religion, Society and the Individual.* New York: Macmillan 1957.

39 Michael Dodson: Explaining Protestant Fundamentalism in Central America. In: Bronislaw Misztal / Anson D. Shupe, Jr. (eds): *Religion and Politics in Comparative Perspective. Revival of Religious Fundamentalism in East and West.* Westport, CT: Praeger 1992; Clifford Hill: Immigrant Sect Development in Britain: A Case of Status Deprivation? In: *Social Compass* 18 (1971), pp. 231–236; id.: From Church to Sect: West Indian Sect Development in Britain. In: *Journal for the Scientific Study of Religion* 10 (1971), pp. 114–123; Andrew G. Walker: From Revival to Restoration: The Emergence of Britain's New Classical Pentecostalism. In: *Social Compass* 32 (1985), pp. 261–271.

40 John L. Gillin: A Contribution to the Sociology of Sects. In: *American Journal of Sociology* 16 (1910), pp. 236–252.

41 Berton H. Kaplan: The Structure of Adaptive Sentiments in Lower Class Religious Groups in Appalachia. In: *Journal of Social Issues* 21 (1965), pp. 126–141.

42 Berton H. Kaplan: The Structure of Adaptive Sentiments in Lower Class Religious Groups in Appalachia. In: *Journal of Social Issues* 21 (1965), pp. 126–141, here p. 136.

43 John D. Photiadis / William Schweiker: Attitudes toward Joining Authoritarian Organizations and Sectarian Churches. In: *Journal for the Scientific Study of Religion* 9 (1970), pp. 227–235.

44 Stephen M. Sales: Economic Threat as a Determinant of Conversion Rates in Authoritarian and Non-Authoritarian Churches. In: *Journal of Personality and Social Psychology* 23 (1972), pp. 420–428.

45 Stewart J. H. McCann: Threatening Times and Fluctuations in American Church Memberships. In: *Personality and Social Psychology Bulletin* 25 (1999), pp. 325–336.

Elmer T. Clark[46] summarized the common characteristics of 200 American sects: (1) Their belief in the speedy ending of this world and the coming of the next where the rich shall be cast down and the humble and meek raised up. (2) The puritan morality in which a virtue is made of frugality, humility and industry, while luxuries and worldly amusements are vices. (3) The stress on simplicity of worship and opposition to expensive belongings. Clark wondered why none of these bodies is interested in earthly social reform.

Liston Pope[47] showed that in the south of the United States, church religiosity was found in the middle and upper classes and sect religiosity in the lower. Walter R. Goldschmidt[48] described Protestant denominationalism in the USA as a reflection of the class structure and social segregation based on class. He suggested that while traditional churches meet the needs of the upper classes, evangelical sects meet working-class needs by offering them a fantasy world. Russell R. Dynes[49] reported that sectarianism as a social attitude, i.e. preference for sect-type religious activities, was correlated with lower socio-economic status. A study of a snake-handling cult in the USA[50] showed that members of this group came from among the poorest whites, described as the rural proletariat of the Southern USA.

Christian Smith and Robert Faris[51] showed that in the United States the members of such groups as Jehovah's Witnesses, Black Baptists, Southern Baptists, and Pentecostalists were lower in income, education, and occupational prestige. Jehovah's Witnesses movement has attracted lower-class individuals all over the world, who seem to react to the complexity and pace of social changes.[52] In terms of beliefs, such groups proclaim an imminent salvation and "tend toward more openly expressive, informal, emotional, and 'Spirit-filled'

46 Elmer T. Clark: *The Small Sects in America.* New York: Abingdon 1965.

47 Liston Pope: *Millhands and Preachers.* New Haven: Yale UP 1942.

48 Walter R Goldschmidt: Class Denominations in Rural California Churches. In: *American Journal of Sociology* 49 (1944), pp. 348–355.

49 Russell R. Dynes: Church-Sect Typology and Socio-Economic Status. In: *American Sociological Review* 20 (1955), pp. 555–560; id.: Rurality, Migration and Sectarianism, In: *Rural Sociology* 21 (1956), pp. 24–28.

50 Weston La Barre: *They Shall Take Up Serpents.* Minneapolis: University of Minnesota Press 1962.

51 Christian Smith / Robert Faris: Socioeconomic Inequality in the American Religious System: An Update and Assessment. In: *Journal for the Scientific Study of Religion* 44 (2005), pp. 95–104.

52 Joseph Bram: Jehovah's Witnesses and the Values of American Culture. In: *Transactions of the New York Academy of Sciences* 19 (1956), pp. 47–54; Werner Cohn: Jehovah's Witnesses as a Proletarian Movement. In: *American Scholar* 24 (1955), pp. 281–298.

styles of worship"[53]. Bryan R. Wilson suggested that "the opportunity for emotional expression in the religious context might be seen as a deflection of concern from social inequalities".[54]

Robyn L. Driskell and Larry Lyon, summarizing a 2005 survey of 1,721 Americans, stated: "We find Evangelical Protestants less likely to be engaged in political and civic activities for reasons [...] that may be tied to beliefs about personal salvation."[55] Pentecostals historically have come from the poor and working class, and scholars have seen the movement as a form of symbolic compensation[56] or protest. Pentecostal rituals, known for their intensity are viewed as a way of reconciling Pentecostals to their social and economic deprivation.

Fundamentalism is a related phenomenon, tied to low income and lower education in individuals.[57] Robbie Duschinsky[58] described worldwide fundamentalist movements as a reaction to the upheavals of modernization and economic insecurity.

Conservative Protestants in the United States, who are likely to follow sectarianism, have been disproportionately female, rural, poor, elderly, and less educated.[59] In terms of wealth accumulation, conservative Protestants have remained at the bottom of the ladder, behind other religious groups, and their situation is unlikely to change. This is to some extent because of their religious beliefs which devalue material rewards.[60] The suggestion is not that poverty leads to religiosity, but that the causality is in the other direction.

53 Smith / Faris: Socioeconomic Inequality, p. 102.

54 Bryan R. Wilson: *Religion in Secular Society*. London: Watts 1966, p. 105.

55 Robyn L. Driskell / Larry Lyon: Assessing the Role of Religious Beliefs on Secular and Spiritual Behavior. In: *Review of Religious Research* 52 (2011), pp. 386–404, here p. 400.

56 Cf. Robert M. Anderson: *Vision of the Disinherited: The Making of American Pentecostalism*. New York: Oxford UP 1979; Jeannette H. Henney: The Shakers of St. Vincent: A Stable Religion. In: Erika Bourguignon (ed.): *Religion, Altered States of Consciousness and Social Change*. Columbus: Ohio State UP 1973, pp. 219–263; Walter J. Hollenweger: *The Pentecostals*. London: SCM 1972; Gary Schwartz: *Sect Ideologies and Social Status*. Chicago: University of Chicago Press 1970; Emilio Willems: *Followers of the New Faith: Culture Change and the Rise of Protestantism in Brazil and Chile*. Nashville: Vanderbilt UP 1967.

57 Barry A. Kosmin / Seymour P. Lachman: *One Nation under God*. New York: Harmony 1993.

58 Robbie Duschinsky: Fundamentalism and the Changing Religious Field. In: *Social Compass* 59 (2012), pp. 21–32.

59 David A. Gay / Christopher G. Ellison: Religious Subcultures and Political Tolerance: Do Denominations still matter? In: *Review of Religious Research* 34 (1993), pp. 311–332.

60 Lisa A. Keister: Conservative Protestants and Wealth: How Religion Perpetuates Asset Poverty. In: *American Journal of Sociology* 113 (2008), pp. 1237–1271.

Race and Caste

Differences of ethnic origin or caste are similar to social class differences, except that in these cases the barriers are almost impossible to cross. Many small sects draw their members from among the very poor and members of minority groups and this seems to be true in many countries. Most findings on the connection between minority ethnicity and religious behavior come from the United States, comparing whites and African-Americans. African-Americans score much higher on all measures of religious activity compared with American whites. Paul Cameron, adopting the Marxian metaphor, simply asserts that "their social situation in the USA requires more 'opiate'".[61]

African-Americans show much higher rates of religious affiliation, as compared to whites.[62] In population surveys dealing with religious experiences, African-Americans reported such experiences more often than whites.[63] In their beliefs, African-Americans are consistently found to be more traditional, and in this respect they parallel poor whites.

When African Americans and whites were compared within the same lower class group, the former were more likely to have sect orientations than their white counterparts,[64] and a major characteristic of Afro-American religion is the existence of small sects and splinter groups, often organized around a charismatic leader.[65] Spiritualist churches among African–Americans were described by Hans A. Baer[66] as a magical reaction to their position in society.

A tragic example of Afro-American millenarianism in the United States was the Peoples Temple, which became the subject of worldwide horror when 918 of its members died in November 1978 in Jonestown, Guyana. It started as a typical, locally organized, working class, congregation, founded in 1956 in Indiana by Jim Jones as the Community National Church. Jones was very

61 Paul Cameron: Personality Differences between Typical Urban Negroes and Whites. In: *Journal of Negro Education* 40 (1971), pp. 66–75, here p. 73.

62 Norval Glenn / Erin Gotard: The Religion of Blacks in the United States: Some Recent Trends and Current Characteristics. In: *American Journal of Sociology* 83 (1977), pp. 443–451.

63 Kurt W Back / Linda B. Bourque: Can Feelings Be Enumerated? In: *Behavioral Science* 15 (1970), pp. 487–496.

64 Edwin Boling: Black and White Religion: A Comparison in the Lower Class. In: *Sociological Analysis* 36 (1975), pp. 73–80.

65 John Dollard: *Caste and Class in a Southern Town*. New York: Doubleday 1949; Norval D. Glenn: Negro Religion and Negro Status in the United States. In: Louis Schneider (ed.): *Religion, Culture and Society*. New York: Wiley 1964, pp. 623–629.

66 Hans A. Baer: *The Black Spiritual Movement: A Religious Response to Racism*. Knoxville: University of Tennessee Press 1984.

active in racial integration when the idea was quite unpopular, and was always very popular with African-Americans. Later the group moved to California. In 1974 it started gradually moving its members to Guyana, in South America, and in 1977 Jones himself and several hundred followers moved there. On November 18, 1978, 918 members died in a mass suicide on orders from Jones, who was among them. It should be noted that most of the members who died with Jones were African-American females.

Religiosity and Mobility

While most of the findings indicate that religious involvement would tend to steer a person away from actions to improve his conditions in this world, religious involvement may lead to improvement via conformity and better adjustment. Moreover, several investigators have suggested that some "deviant" religious movements socialize or re-socialize their members in the direction of the central norms of society, and in this way contribute to an improved adjustment of their members. Benton Johnson[67] and Marion Dearman[68] showed that some sect-type groups help to re-socialize their members according to middle-class values with their emphasis on 'clean living' and asceticism. This in turn helps members in their daily lives and improves their economic situation. John B. Holt[69] similarly described sects as helping in adjustment to the social environment.

Gary Schwartz[70] showed that in some instances religious reactions to deprivation may be instrumental in improving the realistic situation of their followers. In some cases, sect-type movements have led to social mobility and integration. Robert L. Moore stated that dissenting religious movements have provided millions of ordinary Americans with "badges of respectability and [...] a path to upward social mobility".[71] But this is not always true.

At the same time, this kind of adherence to central values is likely to prevent any basic social changes and contributes to the maintenance of the existing

67 Benton Johnson: Do Holiness Sects Socialize in Dominant Values? In: *Social Forces* 39 (1961), pp. 309–317.

68 Marion Dearman: Christ and Conformity: A Study of Pentecostal Values. In: *Journal for the Scientific Study of Religion* 13 (1974), pp. 437–453.

69 Holt: *Holiness Religion*, pp. 740–747.

70 Schwartz: *Sect Ideologies and Social Status.*

71 Robert L. Moore: *Religious Outsiders and the Making of Americans.* New York: Oxford UP 1986, p. 46.

power relations in society. Gerhard E. Lenski[72] found that people who had moved downwards in social status compared with their parents were more interested in religion than those who had kept the same position, and that the latter were more interested than those who had moved upwards.

Twenty-First Century Research

Important research on poverty and religion has been done by Pippa Norris and Ronald Inglehart, who described "the absence of human security as critical for religiosity"[73], and suggested that existential insecurity, which means worrying about your next meal or your next salary, is tied to religiosity. This insecurity explains why religiosity has declined in wealthy nations, and not in poor ones. Moreover, Norris and Inglehart[74] suggested that the personal experience of growing up with economic insecurity creates a stronger religious commitment for life. Economic modernization reduces the need for religious reassurance,[75] and Robert Barro and Rachel McCleary[76] found that economic development leads to lower levels of individual religiosity. Olav Aarts et al.[77] showed that improvements in the quality of life in 26 nations, as measured by the United Nations Human Development Index, had a significant, negative effect on ritual attendance. Ryan T. Cragun and Ronald Lawson[78] suggested that economic development ultimately leads to a secular transition, curtailing the growth of religious groups. A similar survey using data from 114 countries showed that lower rates of employment in agriculture, together with growing income security and equality, led to a decline

72 Gerhard E. Lenski: Social Correlates of Religious Interest. In: *American Sociological Review* 18 (1953), pp. 533–544.

73 Pippa Norris / Ronald Inglehart: *Sacred and Secular: Religion and Politics Worldwide*. Cambridge: Cambridge UP 2004, p. 14.

74 Ibid.

75 Ronald Inglehart / Wayne E. Baker: Modernization, Cultural Change, and the Persistence of Traditional Values. In: *American Sociological Review* 65 (2000), pp. 19–51; Norris / Inglehart: *Sacred and Secular*.

76 Robert Barro / Rachel McCleary: Religion and Economic Growth across Countries. In: *American Sociological Review* 68 (2003), pp. 760–781.

77 Olav Aarts / Ariana Need / Manfred Te Grotenhuis / Nan Dirk de Graaf: Does Duration of Deregulated Religious Markets Affect Church Attendance? Evidence from 26 Religious Markets in Europe and North America between 1981 and 2006. In: *Journal for the Scientific Study of Religion* 49 (2010), pp. 657–672.

78 Ryan T. Cragun / Ronald Lawson: The Secular Transition: The Worldwide Growth of Mormons, Jehovah's Witnesses, and Seventh-Day Adventists. In: *Sociology of Religion* 71 (2010), pp. 349–373.

in religiosity.[79] Inglehart and Norris[80] reported on religiosity in seventy-four nations, divided into three levels of economic development, i. e. agrarian (21), industrial (32), and post-industrial (21). As expected, religiosity level was tied to development.

The prediction that suffering and poverty would lead to higher levels of religiosity has been put to a test by looking at cross-national data. Ritual attendance rates are higher in nations suffering economic inequalities without offering a safety net.[81] In an analysis of 60 nations, Stijn Ruiter and Frank van Tubergen[82] found that religious attendance is primarily affected by personal and societal insecurities. Lower income and being unemployed was also tied to attendance, and there was a high negative correlation between national welfare expenditure and ritual attendance. Mark J. Brandt and Paul J. Henry[83] used data on 216,249 participants in 90 cultures and found that low income and education were tied to higher religiosity. Paulo R. Mourao[84] studied the factors affecting the number of Catholic priests in 38 European countries, covering the period 1950–2006. The findings showed that economic development was the most important determinant of the ratio of Catholic priests to Catholic population, explaining the significant decline between 1950 and 2006.

Frederick Solt, Philip Habel, and Tobin Grant[85] looked at data from countries around the world over two decades and at a time-series analysis of the United States over five decades. They found that economic inequality had a strong positive effect on the religiosity of all members of a society regardless of income. Their conclusion is that greater inequality yields higher religiosity by increasing the extent to which wealthier individuals support religion and have the power to shape the attitudes and beliefs of those with fewer means. Greater economic inequality increases the vulnerability of the poorer

79 Nigel Barber: Country Religiosity Declines as Material Security Increases. In: *Cross-Cultural Research* 47 (2013), pp. 42–50.

80 Ronald Inglehart / Pippa Norris: *Rising Tide: Gender Equality and Cultural Change around the World.* New York: Cambridge UP 2003.

81 Anthony Gill / Erik Lundsgaarde: State Welfare Spending and Religiosity: A Cross-National Analysis. In: *Rationality and Society* 16 (2004), pp. 399–436; Norris / Inglehart: *Sacred and Secular.*

82 Stijn Ruiter / Frank van Tubergen: Religious Attendance in Cross-National Perspective: A Multilevel Analysis of 60 Countries. In: *American Journal of Sociology* 115 (2009), pp. 863–895.

83 Mark J. Brandt / Paul J. Henry: Psychological Defensiveness as a Mechanism Explaining the Relationship between Low Socioeconomic Status and Religiosity. In: *The International Journal for the Psychology of Religion* 22 (2012), pp. 321–332.

84 Paulo R. Mourao: Determinants of the Number of Catholic Priests to Catholics in Europe – An Economic Explanation. In: *Review of Religious Research* 52 (2011), pp. 427–438.

85 Frederick Solt / Philip Habel / Tobin Grant: Economic Inequality, Relative Power, and Religiosity. In: *Social Science Quarterly* 92 (2011), pp. 447–465.

members of a society, and should raise their religiosity level[86]. A survey in 40 nations found that inequality increases religious service attendance, as well as support for the involvement of religious organizations and leaders in politics, and weakens support for secularization, especially among the poor.[87]
The economic insecurity hypothesis has been put to another global test by Ed Diener, Louis Tay, and David G. Myers.[88] They started with what they see as a paradox: if the literature shows that religious individuals report a higher level of subjective well-being (SWB), why is the number of the unaffiliated growing? They found that nations which suffer from poverty, hunger, and low life expectancy were likely to be highly religious. In these nations, religiosity was indeed associated with subjective well-being, so that religious people had a higher SWB in poor, religious nations but not in wealthy, secularized nations.
This finding has been replicated in New Zealand by William J. Hoverd and Chris G. Sibley.[89] The relationship between economic deprivation, religiosity, and SWB was measured in a representative national sample in New Zealand (n=5,984). Individuals living in prosperous areas reported higher levels of SWB regardless of affiliation, while people living in poor neighborhoods reported higher SWB only if they were religiously affiliated.

The Case of the United States

If we find a high level of religiosity in a developed nation, and the best known case is the United States, it may be related to a high level of economic inequality, which leads to insecurity of a majority in the population. The absence of a welfare state (as developed in Europe) may be a primary source for pervasive religiosity in the United States[90]. Georges Delamontagne[91] found that social

86 Norris / Inglehart: *Sacred and Secular.*

87 Ekrem Karakoc / Birol Baskan: Religion in Politics: How Does Inequality Affect Public Secularization? In: *Comparative Political Studies* 45 (2012), pp. 1510–1541.

88 Ed Diener / Louis Tay / David G. Myers: The Religion Paradox: If Religion Makes People Happy, Why Are So Many Dropping Out? In: *Journal of Personality and Social Psychology* 101 (2011), pp. 1278–1290.

89 William J. Hoverd / Chris G Sibley: Religion, Deprivation and Subjective Wellbeing: Testing a Religious Buffering Hypothesis. In: *International Journal of Wellbeing* 3 (2013), pp. 182–196.

90 Franz Hollinger / Max Haller / Adriana Valle-Hollinger: Christian Religion, Society and the State in the Modern World. In: *Innovation: The European Journal of Social Science Research* 20 (2007), pp. 133–157; Johan Verweij / Peter Ester / Rein Nauta: Secularization as an Economic and Cultural Phenomenon: A Cross-National Analysis. In: *Journal for the Scientific Study of Religion* 36 (1997), pp. 309–324.

91 Georges Delamontagne: High Religiosity and Societal Dysfunction in the United States during the First Decade of the Twenty-First Century. In: *Evolutionary Psychology* 8 (2010), pp. 617–657.

inequality (measured by inequalities in education and income) was highly predictive of religiosity in the United States.

Marvin Harris[92] suggested that in the United States, religious awakenings in the twentieth century were the result of frustration with the lack of worldly progress in society. The failure of the American Dream to become reality, has pushed Americans in the direction of fantasy solutions, and Peter Smith[93] interpreted changes in the patterns of religiosity in the United States and Great Britain between 1870 and 1980 as tied to the changing fortunes of the two nations on the world scene. Loss of empire was accompanied by a decline in establishment religiosity in the case of Britain, and by the rise in fundamentalism in the case of the United States.[94]

The correlation between deprivation and religiosity has been found in comparisons of individual states within the United States, with religiosity higher in poorer states. Kurt Gray and Daniel M. Wegner[95] looked at differences in religiosity in individual states, and related them to a "suffering index." The suffering index was based on rates of infant mortality, cancer deaths, infectious disease, violent crime, and environmental pathogens. They found a positive correlation between a state's level of suffering and its religiosity, as measured by reported belief in God (r (48)=.69 p <.001). The connection between suffering and religiosity is demonstrated also by the finding that Americans who report praying often and claim that it brings results are likely to be women, fundamentalists, African-Americans, those with less education and income, the widowed, and the elderly.[96] Similar findings by Joseph O. Baker[97] showed that those with fewer resources and social status pray more often.

92 Marvin Harris: *America Now: The Anthropology of a Changing Culture.* New York: Simon & Schuster 1981.

93 Peter Smith: Anglo-American Religion and Hegemonic Change in the World-System c. 1870–1980. In: *The British Journal of Sociology* 37 (1986), pp. 88–105.

94 Anderson: *Vision of the Disinherited.*

95 Kurt Gray / Daniel M. Wegner: Blaming God for Our Pain: Human Suffering and the Divine Mind. In: *Personality and Social Psychology Review* 14 (2010), pp. 7–16.

96 Kenneth I. Pargament: *The Psychology of Religion and Coping: Theory, Research, Practice.* New York: Guilford 1997.

97 Joseph O. Baker: An Investigation of the Sociological Patterns of Prayer Frequency and Content. In: *Sociology of Religion* 69 (2008), pp. 169–185.

Religiosity and Political Stability

Religion contributes to overall societal and institutional stability by offering relief from various strains and tensions. "Religion not only bids the deprived to accept their lot, but maintains that it is the just outcome of rules that are the best possible, indeed, in some instances divinely inspired"[98]. Social psychologists have studied Just World beliefs, which assert that people generally get what they deserve, and the social order produces the right outcomes. Religions offer ideas that "can encompass an incident of seeming injustice within the larger framework of ultimate justice, [so that] in effect, there are no innocent victims, no injustices, in the ultimate sense of things".[99] The political implications are clear: Just World believers hold conservative views, and there is a marked tendency for religious people to have stronger beliefs in a just world.[100] That effect of religion may serve as an anesthetic for the oppressed, "making the hungry patient, the suffering content, the dying at peace […] feeding […] empty bellies on […] empty words".[101]

Conservatism and conformity, related to religiosity, support the stability of the whole social system. Religious innovations, rather than being disruptive, end up re-integrating potential deviants.[102] Religion as a force for social pacification is very much in evidence in traditional societies. Elizabeth K. Nottingham[103] suggested that the beliefs associated with the Hindu caste system developed to ease its obvious stresses. It is believed that a person's position in the system is merited by her performance in previous incarnations; social discontent is averted by these beliefs. Research on the religious beliefs and behaviors of the Dalit ("untouchables") in India showed that most of them

98 Stark: *The Sociology of Religion*, p. 702.

99 Melvin J. Lerner: *The Belief in a Just World: A Fundamental Illusion*. New York: Plenum 1980, p. 164.

100 Laurent Bègue: Beliefs in Justice and Faith in People: Just World, Religiosity and Interpersonal Trust. In: *Personality and Individual Differences* 32 (2002), pp. 375–382; Claudia Dalbert / Isaac M. Lipkus / Hedvig Sallay / Irene Goch: A Just and an Unjust World: Structure and Validity of Different World Beliefs. In: *Personality and Individual Differences* 30 (2001), pp. 561–577; Adrian Furnham: Belief in a Just World: Research Progress over the Past Decade. In: *Personality and Individual Differences* 34 (2003), pp. 795–817; Richard M. Sorrentino / Jack E. Hardy: Religiousness and Derogation of an Innocent Victim. In: *Journal of Personality* 42 (1974), pp. 372–382; Zick Rubin / Letitia Anne Peplau: Who Believes in a Just World? In: *Journal of Social Issues* 31 (1975), pp. 65–89.

101 Alan Paton: *Cry the Beloved Country: A Story of Comfort in Desolation*. New York: Charles Scribner's Sons 1948, p. 91.

102 Richard J. Bord / Joseph E. Faulkner: *Catholic Charismatics: The Anatomy of a Modern Religious Movement*. University Park, PA: Penn State UP 1983.

103 Elizabeth K. Nottingham: *Religion and Society*. New York: Doubleday 1954.

share the beliefs and religious ideals of the upper castes, though some of their rituals obviously must differ. This consensus enables the caste system, with its self-evident inequalities, to survive.[104]

Pope[105] described a mill town in the southern United States where the mill workers joined small sects which substituted religious status for social status, and the clergy always sided with employers during strikes.[106] In the late twentieth century, it was the conservative Protestant leader Jerry Falwell who stated that "[l]abor unions should study and read the Bible instead of asking for more money. When people get right with God, they are better workers".[107]

Kenneth Scheve and David Stasavage[108] suggested that religious individuals prefer lower levels of wealth redistribution as long as they derive psychological benefits from religion, which buffer individuals against adverse life events and serve as a substitute for the welfare state. John E. Roemer[109] found that when voters had to choose between a secular party favoring the redistribution of wealth and a religious, anti-redistribution, right-wing party, the religious poor will vote for the latter. Anna L. De La O and Jonathan A. Rodden[110] showed that in advanced democracies, religion breaks down the ties between the poor and left-wing parties.

Why do the religious poor vote for parties which oppose distributive justice? One answer may have to do with the kind of issues that divide conservatives and liberals, and are sometimes known as "cultural issues." They cover the status of women, reproductive rights (birth control, abortion), homosexuality, non-marital sexuality, suicide, and euthanasia. Attitudes towards these issues are usually packaged together with economic justice questions in the political

104 Michael Moffatt: *An Untouchable Community in South India: Structure and Consensus*. Princeton: Princeton UP 1979.

105 Liston Pope: Religion and the Class Structure. In: *Annals of the American Academy of Political and Social Science* 256 (1948), pp. 84–91.

106 John R. Earle / Dean D. Knudsen / Donald W. Shriver Jr.: *Spindles and Spires: A Restudy of Religion and Social Change in Gastonia*. Atlanta: Knox 1976.

107 Quoted in Clifford Allen Potts: *Conspirators, Confederates, and Cronies*. Cincinnati, OH: WordTechs 2008, p. 54.

108 Kenneth Scheve / David Stasavage: Religion and Preferences for Social Insurance. In: *Quarterly Journal of Political Science* 1 (2006), pp. 255–286; iid.: The Political Economy of Religion and Social Insurance in the United States, 1910–1939. In: *Studies in American Political Development* 20 (2006), pp. 132–159.

109 John E. Roemer: Why the Poor Do Not Expropriate the Rich: An Old Argument in New Garb. In: *Journal of Public Economics* 70 (1998), pp. 399–424.

110 Anna L. De La O / Jonathan A. Rodden: Does Religion Distract the Poor? Income and Issue Voting around the World. In: *Comparative Political Studies* 41 (2008), pp. 437–476.

platforms of right-wing and left-wing parties. In reaction to "cultural issues", religious voters, who may support the distributive justice principles of the left, support conservative parties in elections.[111] These "cultural issues" may be perceived as tied to the core identity of those who identify as religious above all else. The centrality of sexual issues is intriguing and may be tied to childhood and family experiences.[112]

Conclusion

This survey has shown that wherever we look, we can see that religiosity is indeed tied to poverty and suffering. What emerges from the academic literature reviewed above is that the relationships between religiosity and poverty, measured in various ways, haven't changed over the past two centuries (or more). The realities described already in the early twentieth century are still here, with generalizations still valid. This is despite secularization, which has had significant effects.

Despite all the cultural differences, poor people will find religious language to express their suffering and to find consolation. In other cases, the prayers of the poor and hungry will be asking for security, justice, or revenge. In most cases, these prayers will not change the reality of deprivation. Religion will divert energy from instrumental coping.

I started this article with an expression of concern about the moral meanings of social science research on the correlates of poverty. Reading the literature, one may object to what seems like flattening of the outrage involved. Researchers will break down unmanageable realities into measurable segments. The language of social science, like the language of religion, may act to silence the voice of the victims. It may neutralize the reality of exploitation.

Nevertheless, a close reading of the literature shows that the conventional vocabulary used by academic researchers cannot hide their sensitivity, empathy, and love for the vulnerable. With or without Marxian language, it is clear that those researchers that have chosen to look at this question are not neutral. The choice itself shows that they never intend to deny the reality of suffering or placate those in power.

111 Ibid.

112 Benjamin Beit-Hallahmi: *Psychoanalytic Studies of Religion.* Westport, CT: Greenwood 1996; Benjamin Beit-Hallahmi (ed.): *Psychoanalysis and Theism: Critical Reflections on the Grünbaum Thesis.* Lanham, MD: Aronson 2010.

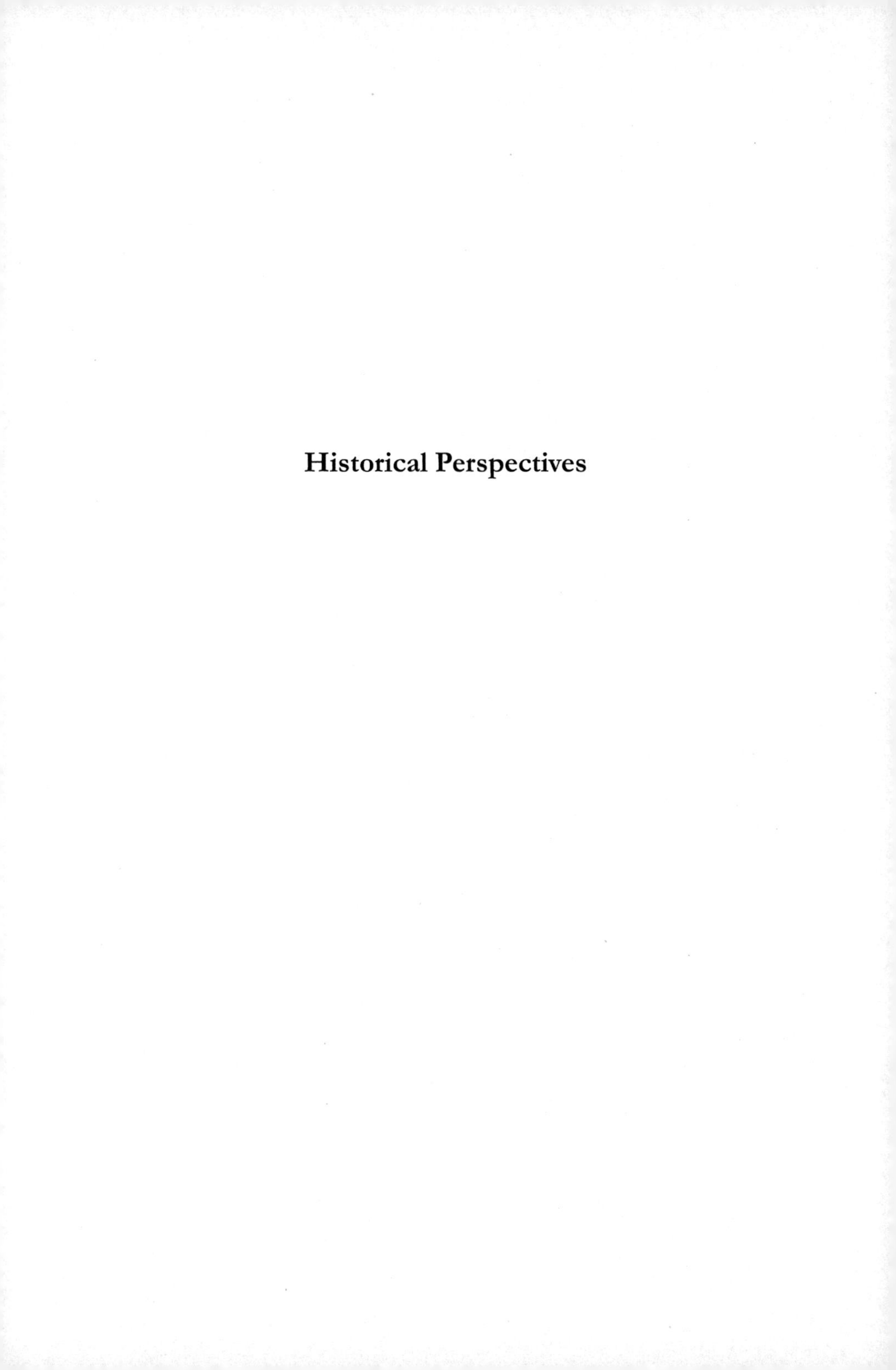

Historical Perspectives

Making Money with Sacredness

The Case of Lucian's *Alexander of Abonuteichos – The False Prophet* between Fact and Fiction

Sabine Müller

In *Alexander* or *the False Prophet* (Ἀλέξανδρος ἢ ψευδόμαντις), the Syrian satirist Lucian of Samosata (ca. 120–180 A.D.) ridicules the success of an oracle founder, depicted as a wicked fraud (γόης). Lucian's story about this crook (mis)using religious beliefs and cultic practices to escape poverty is concerned with different aspects of the interrelationship between religion and poverty. This paper aims to examine the way in which Lucian satirizes the interrelationship between religion and poverty (both material and intellectual).

Alexander founds a cult at Abunoteichos, a small coastal city in the Roman province of Bithynia and Pontus, aiming to swindle his followers out of their money. Epigraphic, numismatic, and archaeological documents testify to the actual existence of the cult devoted to the god Glycon Neos Asclepius, represented as a human-headed serpent with long hair.[1] Established around 140–145 A.D., the cult was a success in many regions of Asia Minor until the early 4th century.[2] Most of the practices Lucian ascribes to Alexander's cult can be paralleled to other oracle shrines and temples of Asclepius of his time.[3] As

Acknowledgements: I would like to thank Jan-Jaap Flinterman, Anneli Purchase, and Kordula Schnegg for their kind help. The translations of *Alexander or the False Prophet* are those of A.M. Harmon (LCL).

1 Angelos Chaniotis: Der Kaiserkult im Osten des Römischen Reiches im Kontext der zeitgenössischen Ritualpraxis. In: Hubert Cancik / Konrad Hitzl (eds): *Die Praxis der Herrscherverehrung in Rom und seinen Provinzen*. Tübingen: Mohr 2003, pp. 3–28, here p. 3; Ulrich Victor: *Lukian von Samosata. Alexandros oder der Lügenprophet.* Leiden: Brill 1997, pp. 1–3; Auguste V.B. Miron: Alexander von Abonuteichos. Zur Geschichte des Orakels des Neos Asklepios Glykon. In: Wolfgang Leschhorn / Auguste V.B. Miron / Andrei Miron (eds): *Hellas und der griechische Osten.* Saarbrücken: Saarbrücker Druckerei u. Verlag 1996, pp. 153–188, here pp. 166–168; Simon Swain: *Hellenism and Empire.* Oxford: Oxford UP 1996, p. 324; Louis Robert: *À travers l'Asie Mineure.* Paris: Boccard 1980, pp. 393–421. On the cult image see Miron: Alexander, pp. 162–168. On the name Glycon (stemming from γλυκύς, a synonym for ἤπιος), see Daniel Ogden: *Alexander the Great. Myth, Genesis and Sexuality.* Exeter: University of Exeter Press 2011, p. 55 (translated as 'Sweety'); Victor: *Lukian*, p. 47 (part of the name Asclepius).

2 Angelos Chaniotis: Old Wine in a New Skin: Tradition and Innovation in the Cult Foundation of Alexander of Abonuteichos. In: *Electrum* 6 (2002), pp. 67–85, here p. 71; Victor: *Lukian*, pp. 7–8.

3 Chaniotis: Old Wine.

the description of Alexander's criminal career is clearly set in a contemporary socio-religious context,[4] additionally emphasized by the "special appearance" of existing individuals,[5] it is regarded as an important document for socio-religious phenomena in the 2nd century A. D.[6] The realistic atmosphere of the narrative underlines the message that, all satiric exaggeration and humoristic ridicule aside, frauds like Alexander existed and were not an uncommon phenomenon. In Lucian's time, oracles boomed, and exercised a considerable social influence.[7] People consulting sanctuaries in the hope of being freed from their problems and fears could easily become victims of fraudsters. However, as the text is the only source for the life of the oracle founder Alexander, the extent to which it is fact or fiction is subject to intense debate.[8] Partly, *Alexander* is seen as a reliable historical biography containing accurate information about the organization of the cult, only slightly distorted by satiric exaggerations.[9] Also, Lucian's claim to have met the false prophet at Abonuteichos[10] is taken as fact.[11] However, this is one of Lucian's ironic

4 Aslak Rostad: The Magician in the Temple: Historicity and Parody in Lucian's *Alexander*. In: *Classica et Mediaevalia* 62 (2011), pp. 207–230, here pp. 215–229.

5 For example, Lucian mentions Severianus, the governor of Cappadocia (Alex. 27), P. Mummius Sisenna Rutilius (cos. suff. 146 A. D.) (Alex. 30, 33–34, 55, 57), Tiberius Julius Eupator, king of the Cimmerian Bosporus (Alex. 57), Avitus (cos. 144) (Alex. 57). A glossary for the abbreviations of ancient sources will be provided at the end of the text.

6 Dorothee Elm: Alexander oder der Lügenprophet. In: Hubert Cancik / Jörg Rüpke (eds): *Römische Reichsreligion und Provinzialreligion*. Erfurt: Digital Druck 2003, pp. 34–46, here p. 40; Victor: *Lukian*, p. vii.

7 Simon Swain: The Three Faces of Lucian. In: Christopher Ligota / Letizia Panizza (eds): *Lucian of Samosata Vivus et Redivivus*. London / Turin: Aragno 2007, pp. 17–44, here p. 42; Chaniotis: Old Wine, p. 67; Miron: Alexander, p. 156; Swain: *Hellenism*, p. 324.

8 Lucian mentions a portrait of Alexander on coins minted in Abonuteichos (Alex. 58). However, no such coin is known. Victor: *Lukian*, p. 170. See also Alexia Petsalis-Diomidis: *Truly Beyond Borders: Aelius Aristides and the Cult of Asklepios*. Oxford: Oxford UP 2010, p. 45.

9 Erik Gunderson: Men of Learning: The Cult of *paideia* in Lucian's *Alexander*. In: Todd C. Penner / Caroline Vander Stichele (eds): *Mapping Gender in Ancient Religious Discourses*. Leiden: Brill 2007, pp. 479–510, here pp. 480–481; Matthew Dickie: Divine Epiphany in Lucian's Account of the Oracle of Alexander of Abonuteichos. In: *Illinois Classical Studies* 29 (2004), pp. 159–182, here pp. 159–160; Chaniotis: Old Wine; Victor: *Lukian*, p. 25; Christopher P. Jones: *Culture and Society in Lucian*. Cambridge, MA / London: Harvard UP 1986, pp. 133–148; Elwyn Jones: *The Concept of the ΘΕΙΟΣ ἈΝΕΡ in the Greco-Roman World With Special Reference to the First Two Centuries A. D.* http://etheses.dur.ac.uk/7937/ (accessed 02.02.2015), p. 213; Arthur D. Nock: Alexander of Abonuteichos. In: *Classical Quarterly* 22 (1928), pp. 160–162.

10 Alex. 55–57.

11 His visit is mainly dated in about 160–163/165 A. D. Gunderson: Men, p. 479, fn. 1; Jan-Jaap Flinterman: The Date of Lucian's Visit to Abonuteichos. In: *Zeitschrift für Papyrologie und Epigraphik* 119 (1997), pp. 280–282; Swain: *Hellenism*, p. 324; Victor: *Lukian*, p. 168; Miron:

self-presentations, obscuring more than exposing the person behind the literary character.[12] Suspiciously, in *Alexander*, the narrator assumes an Epicurean stance while Lucian usually does not take a stand for any philosophical school. Characteristically, Lucian's authorial *personae* are not very heroic, often ambiguous ironic viewers keeping their distance without influencing the outcome of events.[13] Similarly, the narrator in *Alexander* fails to debunk the fraud and ends up fleeing, unable to mobilize the governor of Bithynia and Pontus.[14] However, he also boasts a grand entourage thanks to his friendship with the governor of Cappadocia.[15] Hence, the narrator in *Alexander* is another example of Lucian "capitalising on the notion that exposing oneself to ridicule was a rhetorically potent form of self-representation."[16] Some scholars argue that *Alexander* is primarily a literary parody of traditional motifs surrounding the cultural pattern of the *theios aner* (divine man), while the historical and socio-religious background is secondary.[17] However, this tends to ignore

Alexander, p. 178; Jones: *Culture*, pp. 18–19, 139–140, 145; Otto Weinreich: Alexandros der Lügenprophet und seine Stellung in der Religiosität des II. Jahrhunderts n. Chr. In: *Neue Jahrbücher für das Klassische Altertum* 47 (1921), pp. 129–151, here pp. 131–132.

12 Fabio Berdozzo: *Götter, Mythen und Philosophie: Lukian und die paganen Göttervorstellungen.* Berlin: de Gruyter 2011, p. 213.

13 Sabine Müller: Die Schule(n) der Lügen: Lukian über schlechte Vorbilder und ihre Konsequenzen. In: Christian Hoffstadt / Sabine Müller (eds): *Von Lehrerkritik bis Lehrermord.* Bochum / Freiburg: Projekt 2013, pp. 25–37, here p. 27; Robert Bracht Branham: *Unruly Eloquence: Lucian and the Comedy of Traditions.* Cambridge, MA / London: Harvard UP 1989, p. 34.

14 Alex. 53–57; Petsalis-Diomidis: *Truly Beyond Borders*, p. 46; Oliver Overwien: Lukian als Literat, Lukian als Feind. In: *Rheinisches Museum für Altertumskunde* 149 (2006), pp. 185–213, here pp. 210–211. On the narrator in *Alexander* see Bracht Branham: *Unruly Eloquence*, pp. 179–210.

15 Alex. 55.

16 Keith Sidwell: The Dead Philosopher's Society: New Thoughts on Lucian's *Piscator* and Eupolis' *Demes*. In: Adam Bartley (ed.): *A Lucian for Our Times.* Cambridge: Cambridge Scholars 2009, pp. 109–118, here p. 111.

17 Jens Gerlach: Die Figur des Scharlatans bei Lukian. In: Peter Pilhofer / Manuel Baumbach / Jens Gerlach (eds): *Lukian: Der Tod des Peregrinos: Ein Scharlatan auf dem Scheiterhaufen.* Darmstadt: WBG 2005, pp. 151–197; Bracht Branham: *Unruly Eloquence*, pp. 181–210; Graham Anderson: *Studies in Lucian's Comic Fiction.* Leiden: Brill 1976, p. 21; Jacques Bompaire: *Lucien Écrivain.* Paris: Boccard 1958, pp. 480–482. On the role-model of the *theios aner* Erkki Koskenniemi: Apollonius of Tyana: A Typical θεῖος ἀνήρ? In: *Journal of Biblical Literature* 117 (1998), pp. 455–467, here pp. 456–458; Jan-Jaap Flinterman: The Ubiquitous 'Divine Man'. In: *Numen* 43 (1996), pp. 82–96, here p. 82; Barry Blackburn: *Theios aner and the Markan Miracle Traditions.* Tübingen: Mohr 1991, pp. 88–90, 96; Charles H. Talbert: The Concept of Immortals in Mediterranean Antiquity. In: *Journal of Biblical Literature* 94 (1975), pp. 419–436, here pp. 419, 425; Jones: *Concept.* Its existence is debated as there is no fixed ancient concept (Koskienniemi: Apollonius of Tyana, p. 456–460). However, there existed a "common fund" (Jones: *Concept*, p. 206) of ideas. Barbara Szlagor: *Verflochtene Bilder: Lukians Porträtierung „göttlicher Männer".* Trier: Wissenschaftlicher Verlag 2005, pp. 13–17; Flinterman: Divine Man, pp. 89, 93.

the function of satire that takes aim at aspects of real life, which would not work without this authentic background.[18] Therefore, it is more plausible to argue for a compromise in favor of "an interplay between historicity and comedy."[19]

The following examination is based on the assumption that Lucian's Alexander was not a historical person but a literary figure: a caricature of the image(s) associated in the collective memory with persons linked with perceptions of the phenomenon of the *theios aner*[20] such as oracle founders, priests, or miracle-workers. It explains why Lucian, who usually ridicules types and images rather than individuals,[21] ascribes the whole range of characteristics connected with the phenomenon of the *theios aner* to Alexander.

Generally viewing oracles, cults, and religious beliefs with ridicule and skepticism,[22] Lucian bases his satire on real religious practices of his time, choosing as an example a successful cult from his own cultural realm.[23] He was a Syrian from the former kingdom of Commagene. His choice might also have been influenced by his own negative experience with the effects of useless oracles during the "Antonine Plague." Lucian's account that the oracle of Glycon advised putting a verse about Phoebus Apollon over the doorway as a charm against the plague might be authentic. He comments: "but in most cases it had the contrary result […]. [P]eople neglected precautions because of their confidence in the line and lived too carelessly".[24]

18 Ulrich Rütten: *Phantasie und Lachkultur. Lukians Wahre Geschichten.* Tübingen: Narr 1997, pp. 42–43.

19 Rostad: Magician, p. 208. Sabine Müller: Trügerische Bilder? Lukians Umgang mit Tyrannen- und Orienttopoi in seinen Hadesszenen. In: *Gymnasium* 120 (2013), pp. 169–192, here pp. 114–115; Petsalis-Diomidis: *Truly Beyond Borders*, p. 11; Christian Oesterheld: Rezension zu Ulrich Victor, Lukian von Samosata. Alexandros. In: *Göttinger Forum für Altertumswissenschaft* 4 (2001), pp. 1177–1179, here p. 1178.

20 In Lucian's words: with the appearance as θεοπρεπής, godlike: Alex. 3.

21 Bracht Branham: *Unruly Eloquence*, p. 101.

22 Elm: Alexander, p. 44; Miron: Alexander, p. 187; Jones: *Culture*, pp. 24, 33, 42–45; Jones: *Concept*, p. 207.

23 Rostad: Magician, p. 214.

24 Alex. 36; Sabine Müller: Lukian, Ammianus Marcellinus, der Ausbruch der Antoninischen Pest und die literarische Tradition von Götterzorn und Krankheit. In: Christian Hoffstadt / Sabine Müller / Melanie Möller / Michael Nagenborg / Franz Peschke (eds): *Zwischen Vorsorge und Schicksal. Über die Beherrschbarkeit des Körpers in der Medizin.* Bochum / Freiburg: Projekt 2014, pp. 117–134, here pp. 117–118; Fritz Graf: The Oracle and the Image: Returning to Some Oracles from Clarus. In: *Zeitschrift für Papyrologie und Epigraphik* 160 (2007), pp. 113–119; Zsuzsanna Varhelyi: Magic, Religion and Syncretism at the Oracle of Clarus. In: Sulochana Asirvatham / Corinne O. Pache / John Watrous (eds): *Between Magic and Religion.* Lanham: Bowman & Littlefield 2001, pp. 11–29, here pp. 16–23.

The fake prophet is named Alexander for a reason. Ostentatiously, in his introduction, Lucian alludes to Arrian. Ironically echoing Arrian's proud self-representation in his *Anabasis Alexandrou* as a highly renowned member of the intellectual and political elite and the only one qualified to write the true history of Alexander[25], Lucian claims that he and Arrian both wrote biographies of criminals:

> [H]e thought fit […] to record the life of Tilliborus, the brigand. In our case, however, we shall commemorate a far more savage brigand, since our hero […] instead of […] harrying a few of the more deserted districts of Asia, he filled the whole Roman Empire […] with his brigandage.[26]

Arrian's alleged biography of a robber terrorizing Asia is not attested elsewhere and will be an ironic allusion to Arrian's hero Alexander in accordance with the latter's reception as a brigand by Roman writers.[27] Given this, the name of the false prophet chosen by Lucian explicitly hints at another aspect of the text: ridiculing Arrian's treatment of an iconic figure in his *Anabasis*.[28] Consequently, the portrait of the *pseudomantis* Alexander is more than "an inversion of encomiastic portrayals of Alexander"[29]: By paralleling

25 An. 1.12.4–5.

26 Alex. 2.

27 Sen. De ben. 1.13.3; Ep. 94.62; Luc. Phars. 10.20–21. Müller: Trügerische Bilder, pp. 186–187; Dorothee Elm: Die Inszenierung des Betruges und seiner Entlarvung. In: Ead. / Jörg Rüpke / Katharina Waldner (eds): *Texte als Medium und Reflexion von Religion im römischen Reich*. Stuttgart: Steiner 2006, pp. 141–157, here p. 155; Henri Tonnet: *Recherches sur Arrien*, vol. I. Amsterdam: Hakkert 1988, pp. 73, 83; Gerhard Wirth: Anmerkungen zur Arrian-Biographie: Appian – Arrian – Lukian. In: *Historia* 13 (1964), pp. 209–245, here p. 233. Contra: Swain: *Hellenism*, p. 326, fn. 101.

28 There are other indicators. Describing his meeting with Alexander, Lucian claims to be a friend of the governor of Cappadocia (Alex. 55). Decades before, in the 130s, Arrian was the governor of Cappadocia. He commemorated this in his *Periplus Ponti Euxini*, thereby distinguishing himself as a connoisseur of Greek culture (Sabine Müller: Arrian and Visual Arts. In: *Journal of Ancient Civilizations* 29 (2014), pp. 87–101). Describing his voyage of inspection along the coast of the Black Sea, he continuously refers to Greek literature and calls himself (the new) Xenophon (Per. 1.1; 1.2; 2.3; 3.2; 8.2; 11.1; 13.5; 14.4–5; 15.1; 16.3; 25.1). Fleeing from Alexander, Lucian comments that the city where he stops was mentioned by Homer (Alex. 57). This makes sense as a parody of Arrian's *Periplus*. He also states that he travelled in company of an otherwise unmentioned Xenophon (Alex. 56). Harmon takes him for a slave or freedman (LCL, p. 247, n. 1). But it may well be another ironic response to Arrian's *habitus*. Contra Ogden: *Alexander*, p. 56, supposing that the historical oracle founder may have adapted the name and some of the imagery of Alexander. However, also the form of *Alexander* reminds of the *Anabasis*: a biography resembling the genre of the *praxeis* (Jones: *Concept*, p. 214).

29 Tim Whitmarsh: *The Second Sophistic*. Oxford: Oxford UP 2005, p. 68, fn. 43. Gerlach: Figur, p. 179, fn. 73. Gunderson: Men, p. 488, characterizes the false prophet also as "something of a conqueror." Müller: Trügerische Bilder, p. 185.

his authorial *persona* with Arrian and associating *Alexander* with his writings, Lucian reverses Arrian's way of approaching an iconic figure. While Arrian claims to write the truth by creating an idealized iconic portrait by also highlighting his own skills as a historiographer, Lucian strips off the "godlike" features of his Alexander and destroys the iconic image. This is a humorous contradiction to the failure of his narrator *persona* to unmask the fraud.
Not surprisingly, there are several ironic references to Alexander III in *Alexander*, predominantly concerned with charges of his hubristic longing for divinity which Arrian tried to neutralize.[30] Arrian ends his *Anabasis* claiming that it was written for "the good of mankind" and divinely supported like Alexander's deeds.[31] Lucian's *Alexander* ends: "I think too that to its readers the writing will seem to have some usefulness, refuting as it does certain falsehoods and confirming certain truths in the minds of all men of sense".[32] The difference is significant: The claim of divine protection is missing and, according to Lucian, his text will only be useful to people of sense, not to 'mankind'.

From Rags to Riches: The Rise and False *Theios Aner*

In Lucian's portrayal of the sham oracle founder Alexander, poverty is a key issue. Alexander's career in the religion business even has roots in his poverty. Originally, he was promising and talented: "In understanding, quick-wittedness, and penetration he was far beyond everyone else; and activity of mind, readiness to learn, retentiveness, natural aptitude for studies – all these qualities were his, in every case to the full".[33] However, due to his humble origins[34], he could not afford a proper education to support his qualities. Instead, Alexander makes a living as a boy prostitute: "While he was still a mere boy (μειράκιον), and a very handsome one (πάνυ ὡραῖον) [...], he trafficked freely in his attractiveness and sold his company to those who sought it".[35] This

30 Luc. Alex. 1; 6; 7 (Plut. Alex. 2.4; Just. 11.11; Arr. an. 4.10.2); 16 (Plut. Alex. 76.4; Arr. an. 7.26.1); 41 (indirect). Müller: Trügerische Bilder, pp. 184–187; Ogden: *Alexander*, p. 44; Petsalis-Diomidis: *Truly Beyond Borders*, p. 45; Daniel Ogden: Lucian, Glycon, and the Two Alexanders. In: Mustafa Çevik (ed.): *International Symposium on Lucianus of Samosata.* Adiyaman: Adiyaman University 2009, pp. 279–300; Jones: *Culture*, pp. 133, 136. Arr. an. 3, 3, 2; 7, 29, 3–4. On the importance of Alexander III in the *Second Sophistic* see Whitmarsh: *The Second Sophistic*, p. 66.

31 An. 7, 30, 3.

32 Alex. 61.

33 Alex. 4.

34 Alex. 11.

35 Alex. 5.

episode, often glossed over, is a key factor.[36] It marks Alexander's early corruption due to a lack of proper *paideia*. Even worse, Alexander's occupation as a teenage prostitute leads to an alternative "education": an apprenticeship as a professional fraud.

> Among others, he had an admirer (ἐραστὴς) who was a quack, one of those who advertise enchantments, miraculous incantations, charms for your love-affairs [...]. As this man saw that he was an apt lad, more than ready to assist him in his affairs, and that the boy was quite as much enamored with his roguery as he with the boy's beauty, he gave him a thorough education (ἐξεπαίδευσέ) and constantly made use of him as helper, servant and acolyte.[37]

This comic inversion of the Platonic ideal of the pedagogic *eros* is more than a topical invective. It hints at what Lucian seems to regard as the mark of true *paideia*: the improvement of the pupil. According to Socrates' lessons in Plato (who plays a major role in Lucian's œuvre), erotic reciprocity serves to improve the *eromenos* morally and intellectually, while the teacher-lover cares for him as a kindred soul[38] enabling him to become as good as possible.[39] The good *erastes* is attracted by his beloved's physical beauty but prefers the beauty of his soul.[40] The aim of the relationship is to make both partners better men (and citizens): "the two lovers will construct a social space in which they will be most able to satisfy their desire to possess the good."[41] Overcoming a lofty immaterial poverty plays a role, too: The lovers want to "replace their poverty with plenty in the ultimate hope of resembling the divine."[42] This is regarded as a better prize than material payment for the teacher. Ironically, Lucian shows the perversion of this ideal.[43] Alexander and his *erastes* see themselves

36 James Jope: Lucian's Triumphant *Cinaedus* and Rogue Lovers. In: *Helios* 36 (2009), pp. 55–64, here p. 61.

37 Alex. 5.

38 Phaedr. 255 D.

39 Phaedr. 243 E–257 B; Marguerite Johnson: The Role of Eros in Improving the Pupil. In: Marguerite Johnson / Harold Tarrant (eds): *Alcibiades and the Socratic Lover-Educator*. Bristol: Bristol Classical 2012, pp. 7–29; Anthony Hooper: The Dual-Role Philosophers. In: Ibid., pp. 107–117, here pp. 107–108, 112. On the importance of Plato in Lucian's œuvre Berdozzo: *Götter*, pp. 191, 202; Bracht Branham: *Unruly Eloquence*, pp. 67–80.

40 Plat. Alc. 135 E; Phaedr. 253 C–256 E; Symp. 215 A–219 D; Dougal Blyth: Socratic and Platonic Models of Love. In: Johnson / Tarrant (eds): *Alcibiades and the Socratic Lover-Educator*, pp. 30–44, here pp. 40–41.

41 Hooper: The Dual-Role Philosophers, p. 107.

42 Ibid., p. 108.

43 Petsalis-Diomidis: *Truly Beyond Borders*, p. 56; Gunderson: Men, pp. 499–501; Jope: Lucian's Triumphant *Cinaedus*, pp. 61–63. This kind of misunderstanding of the Socratic pedagogic *eros* is a common theme in Lucian's œuvre serving to reveal the vices of pseudo-authorities (Berdozzo: *Götter*, pp. 200–201).

in each other as mirror-images like the Socratic lovers do,[44] but they become fellows in crime instead of accompanying each other in the pursuit of the good.[45] As far as erotic reciprocity is concerned, Alexander is keen on his lover's criminal lessons while the man is mad for his body. The results of this bad education are clear: "But he made the worst possible use of them and with these noble instruments at his service soon became the most perfect rascal of all those who have been notorious far and wide for villainy".[46] So, Lucian's narrative implies that the great oracle swindle has roots in Alexander's early material poverty that led to a bad education and moral poverty.

The corrupt teacher also provides the link to the religious sphere and perceptions of the *theios aner*. Lucian mentions that the man was a disciple of the famous Neo-Pythagorean Apollonius of Tyana "who knew his whole bag of tricks".[47] While Lucian characterizes him as another notorious fraud, Apollonius was mainly commemorated as an iconic ascetic philosopher with wondrous power associated with the diverse cultural pattern of the wonder-working *theios aner*, the 'divine man' favored by the gods.[48] Such a man was assumed to display the divine presence because of his special insight into the superhuman sphere and to be possessed of divine wisdom.[49]

Thanks to this particular background of the corrupt physician from Tyana, his 'pupil' Alexander is able to help himself when the elder man's death coincides with the fading of his commercially useful flower of youth.[50] However, he was clearly not forced to give up this business immediately. Still beautiful enough to charm at least an elderly woman from Macedonia, he travels

44 Plat. Phaedr. 255 D.

45 Plat. Alc. 124 B–C.

46 Alex. 4.

47 Alex. 5.

48 James A. Francis 2003: Living Icons. Tracing a Motif in Verbal and Visual Representation from the Second to Fourth Centuries C.E. In: *American Journal of Philology* 124 (2003), pp. 575–600, here pp. 580, 582–584; Chaniotis: Old Wine, p. 69; Jones: *Concept*, pp. 206, 216. He was depicted this way by Philostratus in his *Life of Apollonius of Tyana* (3rd century A.D.). See also the critical arguments by Koskenniemi: Apollonius of Tyana, pp. 460–467.

49 Gerlach: Figur; Bracht Branham: *Unruly Eloquence*, pp. 181–210; Anderson: Studies, p. 21; Bompaire: *Lucien Écrivain*, pp. 480–482. On the role-model of the *theios aner* Koskenniemi: Apollonius of Tyana, pp. 456–458; Flinterman: Divine Man, p. 82; Blackburn: *Theios aner*, pp. 88–90, 96; Talbert: Concept, pp. 419, 425; Jones: *Concept*. Its existence is debated as there is no fixed ancient concept visible (Koskienniemi: Apollonius of Tyana, p. 456–460). However, it is obvious that there existed a "common fund" (Jones: *Concept*, p. 206). Szlagor: *Verflochtene Bilder*, pp. 13–17; Flinterman: Divine Man, pp. 89, 93.

50 Alex. 6.

at her expense with her and a fellow crook to her motherland. Having the idea of their life, they buy a tame serpent, "the finest, for a few obols," at Pella.[51] Thus, the beginnings of the cult are as humble as they are dubious: A corrupted gigolo and his accomplice buy an inexpensive reptile.[52] Probably, Alexander earned the obols for this principle part of his great swindle by selling himself to the old lady. However, this is his ticket into religious 'big business': "they concocted the project of founding a prophetic shrine, an oracle, hoping that if they should succeed in it, they would at once be rich and prosperous".[53]

Back in Asia Minor, Alexander sets himself up as the *prophetes* (interpreter) of the oracles purported to come from Glycon. This divinity was proclaimed to be a reincarnation of the most worshipped ancient healing-god, Asclepius, in whose cult the snake was traditionally prominent.[54] Announced by fake prophecies and accompanied by special effects, Alexander celebrates the birth of the divine epiphany in his Paphlagonian hometown of Abonuteichos.[55] The New Asclepius is in fact the tame Macedonian serpent with a humanoid head with long hair provided by a puppet.[56] To cover up the fake, Alexander exhibits the manipulated reptile only in a darkened room. Hedging himself around with various forms of sanctity underscored by Lucian by the repeated metaphor of theatrical performances,[57] he presents himself as the descendant of Asclepius and Perseus.[58]

Cleverly responding to diverse needs, his sanctuary provides "all in one": Alexander claims that "he made predictions, discovered fugitive slaves, detected thieves and robbers, caused treasures to be dug up, healed the sick, and in some cases had actually raised the dead".[59] Hence, the cult is successful

51 Alex. 7.

52 In any case, the serpent is cheaper than one of Alexander's oracles which cost 1 drachma and 2 obols (Luc. Alex. 23).

53 Alex. 8.

54 Chaniotis: Old Wine, p. 74.

55 Alex. 10–14.

56 Luc. Alex. 12, 15–16.

57 Petsalis-Diomidis: *Truly Beyond Borders*, p. 57; Serena Zweimüller: *Lukian Rhetorum praeceptor. Einleitung, Text und Kommentar*. Göttingen: Vandenhoeck & Ruprecht 2008, pp. 131, 133–134, 140; Chaniotis: Old Wine, p. 80.

58 Alex. 11–12; On Perseus as the link to the Achaemenids see Chaniotis: Old Wine, p. 79. On the link to the dynasty of Mithradates VI of Pontus see Nock: Alexander, p. 161.

59 Alex. 24; Angelos Chaniotis: Wie (er)findet man Rituale für einen neuen Kult? http://www.ub.uni-heidelberg.de/archiv/5103 (accessed 22.02.2015); Chaniotis: Old Wine, p. 71; Victor: *Lukian*, p. 38–40.

as an oracular site, a healing center, and a kind of mystery cult combining traditional and new elements.[60] It is supported even by members of leading Roman circles like P. Mummius Sisenna Rutilianus.[61] Alexander makes him marry his daughter, claiming that Glycon recommended this marriage.[62] Thus, from a boy prostitute he makes his way into high society: the perversion of the role model of the self-made man.

Lucian hints that Alexander's pose as a *theios aner* was an important factor in his career.[63] He seduces his followers (not only metaphorically) with his good looks and charms. In outward appearance, he equals general perceptions of men thought to be divine favorites and to possess supernatural powers. However, his looks were just another illusion, partly provided by a theatrical requisite:

> [H]e was tall and handsome (καλός) in appearance and really godlike (θεοπρεπής); his skin was fair, his beard not very thick, his long hair was in part natural, in part false, but very similar, so that most people did not detect that it was not his own. His eyes shone with a great glow of fervour and enthusiasm; his voice was at once very sweet and very clear; and in a word, no fault could be found with him in any respect as far as all that went. Such, then, was his outward appearance; but his soul and his mind – O Heracles Forfender![64]

In a time when "issues of visual representation were on the mind of writers" as well as the question how an image works,[65] Lucian points out the corrupting and mind-blowing power of images set against a sacral background:

> He now wore his hair long, had falling ringlets, dressed in a parti-colored tunic of white and purple, with a white cloak over it, and carried a falchion like that of Perseus, from whom he claimed descent on his mother's side. And although those miserable Paphlagonians knew that both his parents were obscure, humble folk, they believed in the oracle.[66]

A major element of the sacralized iconography, the distinctively long hair worn both by Glycon and his prophet is a key feature of Lucian's parody of

60 Chaniotis: Old Wine, p. 68; Georg Luck: Witches and Sorcerers in Classical Literature. In: Valerie I. J. Flint (ed.): *Witchcraft and Magic in Europe: Ancient Greece and Rome.* London: A&C Black 1999, pp. 91–157, here pp. 146–147.

61 Alex. 30–31; PIR² M 711.

62 Alex. 35.

63 Blackburn: *Theios aner*, pp. 88–90; Jones: *Concept*, pp. 208 ("the prophetic, ecstatic type"), 213–221.

64 Alex. 3.

65 Francis: Living Icons, pp. 582, 588. See also Jones: *Concept*, p. 217.

66 Alex. 11.

Alexander, as a θεοπρεπής also associated with philosophers and intellectuals of his time.[67] Alexander's fake hair is mentioned three times.[68] Notably, Lucian refers to it when he tries to debunk the fraud[69]: He asks the oracle whether Alexander was bald (and of course, receives only a cryptic answer). Lucian's motive is clear: By trying to prove that one determinative of Alexander's outward resemblance to popular perceptions of 'divine men' is fake, he hopes to make clear that all self-fashioning is a show.

The following account of Alexander's deeds as a prophet provides the recipient with a detailed catalogue of the (inverted) features of the cultural pattern of the *theios aner*, showing that "Lucian was aware how a θεῖος ἀνήρ, genuine or otherwise, was conceived in the popular eye".[70] Ironically exaggerated, his fraud tries to live up to all of the major elements of such an image.

Generally, individuals associated with this phenomenon were perceived as benefactors to mankind, often as great teachers and symbols of virtue and cultural and social values.[71] Common features include an unusual parentage, great intellect and rationality early in their childhood, an extraordinary life, divine wisdom, and deep insight into human nature. Their inner virtues are mirrored by the beauty (χάρις) of their bodies and voices. They treat their enemies with merciful patience. They are often ascetics, become visible as cult founders, prophets, sages or wonder workers, and stand up for peace and try to save their followers by convincing them to live a better life. Firmly believing in their own mission to heal the world (or at least their disciples), they display their divine predestination through prophetic utterances, miracles, extraordinary virtue, or wisdom. The climax of such an extraordinary life is often heavenly ascent at the moment of death.[72]

As a counter-image, Lucian's Alexander bestows benefactions primarily on himself and cheats on the shrine's visitors with his fabricated snake, false

67 Szlagor: *Verflochtene Bilder*, p. 37; Chaniotis: Old Wine, p. 70. Particularly, the long hair connects him with Pythagoras. Victor: *Lukian*, p. 167: A prophet was expected to suit the ideals of perfect masculine beauty.

68 Alex. 3, 53, 59.

69 Alex. 53.

70 Jones: *Concept*, p. 214. See also Petsalis-Diomidis: *Truly Beyond Borders*, p. 47; Szlagor: *Verflochtene Bilder*, pp. 35–86; Elm: Alexander, p. 44. On the historical background of the self-fashioning of priests and prophets see Beate Dignas: Greek Priests in the First Three Centuries CE. In: Ead. / Robert Parker / Guy G. Strousma (eds): *Priests and Prophets among Pagans, Jews and Christians*. Leuven: Peeters 2013, pp. 80–111.

71 Talbert: Concept, p. 425.

72 Szlagor: *Verflochtene Bilder*, pp. 27–34; John Nolland: Grace as Power. In: *Novum Testamentum* 28 (1986), pp. 26–31; Talbert: Concept, pp. 419–425; Blackburn: *Theios aner*.

predictions, nonsense oracles, and staged shows. He harms the people with useless remedies like his own healing medium made of bear's fat,[73] and blackmails them with the content of their questions. Hence, he is a symbol of trickery, malice, and villainy. His claims of divine descent contradict the obscure origins of his parents. He possesses inner qualities but instead uses his cleverness and insight into human nature to further his villainy. His beauty is partly fake and contradicts his inner corruption. He pursues his enemies hatefully.[74] Instead of living an ascetic life, Alexander pursues his aim to become rich and indulges in sexual excesses. With regards to materialism, he cleverly transfers the ascetic ideal to Glycon:

> So there was a hustling and a bustling from every side, with sacrifices and votive offerings – and twice as much for the prophet and the disciple of the god. For this oracle had also come out: 'Honour I bid you to give my faithful servant, the prophet / No great store do I set upon riches, but much on the prophet.'[75]

Hence, while the snake-god lived in conformity with any expectations of asceticism, his prophet was excused by the oracle.

Alexander's lifestyle was promiscuous. Again, his sexual morality is an important factor in his portrayal.[76] Lucian reveals the hypocrisy of his claims to maintain high moral standards: Alexander commits adultery with the worshippers' wives and is the first to break his own rule of abstaining from sexual intercourse with boys. He abuses the most beautiful male children of his noblest followers (sent to him as his choir boys), imprisoning them as his sex slaves.[77] A notion of an "ironic aura of sanctity"[78] surrounds Alexander's claim of having a daughter by the moon goddess Selene. The idea that the child was the product of a *hieros gamos* underlines Alexander's self-fashioning as a divine favorite and gives the story of the encounter between human and divine a real touch.

73 Alex. 22.

74 Alex. 25, 38, 56.

75 Alex. 24.

76 On sex in *Alexander* see Gunderson: Men, pp. 499–501.

77 Alex. 41–42; Gunderson: Men, p. 49, thinks that this is a sexualized metaphor: While Alexander uses the boys literally like sex slaves, he does this metaphorically to Rutilianus. Richard Hawley: 'Give Me a Thousand Kisses': The Kiss, Identity, and Power in Greek and Roman Antiquity. http://www.leeds.ac.uk/classics/lics/ (accessed 14.02.2015), points out that Lucian emphasizes Alexander's hypocrisy by describing the kiss of greeting he expects from his visitors (Alex. 41): His desire for young boys is covered up by his practice of not welcome-kissing on the lips anyone over 18 years of age. It seems to be a parody of the formal kiss of greeting or farewell attested in Greek historiography for Cyrus II (Xen. Cyr. 1.4.27–28) and Alexander III (Plut. Alex. 54.3–6).

78 Jones: *Concept*, p. 220.

Lucian sarcastically compares Alexander to Selene's lover Endymion,[79] the symbol of the bloom of youth. Alexander, however, was at an age that made the comparison awkward.

For an oracle founder posing as a savior whose "teacher" was associated with the iconic image of an ascetic philosopher, promiscuity seems particularly inappropriate, especially as sexual continence or abstinence was prominent in the cult of Asclepius. It was supposed that mental and physical purity was required to come into contact with the god, especially in incubation.[80] According to Lucian, in contrast to the usual practice of letting the worshippers sleep in the sanctuary to have divinely inspired dreams, only Alexander himself contacted the god in incubation.[81] Hence, a promiscuous lifestyle appears as a clear contradiction to his role as Glycon's prophet, marking him as an out-and-out charlatan.

The fake character of Alexander's prophetic utterances and divine protection is highlighted by the last chapter of his career, suiting the ancient literary device that the circumstances of an individual's death should reflect their life. Lucian ridicules Alexander's hubristic claim of ascending to heaven (and becoming immortal):

> In spite of his prediction in an oracle that he was fated to live 150 years and then die by a stroke of lightning, he met a most wretched end before reaching the age of 70 […] for his leg became mortified quite to the groin and was infested with maggots.[82]

The Prophet, the Worshippers, and Poverty

Despite Lucian's sarcasm, he makes it clear that Alexander dies as a man who successfully escaped from poverty. The temple was prosperous and expanded from a one-man show into a considerable business with a great number of cult personnel, including assistants, servants, spies, writers and custodians of oracles, clerks, and sealers.[83] When the shrine boomed, Alexander was not content with selling false oracles, useless amulets, ointments, and charms; he

79 Alex. 39; Nock: Alexander, p. 161, fn. 4.

80 Chaniotis: Old Wine, p. 76; Marc Kleijwegt: Beans, Baths and the Barber … A Sacred Law from Thuburbo Maius. In: *Antiquités Africaines* 30 (1994), pp. 209–220, here pp. 219–220. Epigraphic evidence from the 2nd century A. D. attests to such sacred laws in cults of Asclepius.

81 Alex. 49.

82 Alex. 59; Talbert: Concept, p. 429. It seems to be a significant death: Imitating Pythagoras, Alexander exposed a golden thigh (Ael. VH 2.26). Actually, it was a piece of gilded leather (Alex. 40). It will be no coincidence that he died of an infected leg. Similarly, his accomplice Cocconas died bitten by a snake (Alex. 10).

83 Alex. 23, 36–37.

also employed interpreters who demanded large fees from visitors for explaining Glycon's oracles. Lucian leaves no doubt that these were deliberately cryptic to make the clients consult the interpreters: "this task of theirs was subject to a levy; the expounders paid Alexander an Attic talent each".[84]
The sanctuary attracted the masses who first spread its fame and the rich who followed. The so-called self-spoken (αὐτόφωνοι) oracles were reserved for the prosperous upper class.[85] Allegedly, the serpent answered the questions with a human voice (while actually one of Alexander's accomplices spoke through a crane's windpipe attached to its head). However, the majority of visitors were cheated in a less extravagant way. They handed in sealed rolls of paper containing individual questions which Alexander secretly read before fixing the broken seals.[86] Lucian reports:

> A prize had been fixed for each oracle, a drachma and two obols. Do not think that it was low, my friend, or that the revenue from this source was scanty! He gleaned as much as seventy or eighty thousand a year since men were so greedy as to send in ten and fifteen questions each.[87]

Opinions differ over whether this was a large prize.[88] Lucian seems to indicate that it was not. The charms Alexander sold against the plague seem to have been another cheap variant.[89]
Lucian's narrative implies that the secret of the cult's success was its mass compatibility.[90] A "crowd of heterogeneous humanity, excited, wonder-struck in advance, agog with hopes"[91] was attracted to the sanctuary for four main reasons: the wide range of its functions; the chance to see and even touch the living snake-god[92]; the possibility to get in (sometimes very) close touch with the prophet; and the carefully staged performances. Alexander knew how to put on an impressive show, astonish the crowd and distinguish himself as

84 Alex. 49.
85 Alex. 26–27.
86 Alex. 19.
87 Alex. 23.
88 High prize: Harmon, LCL, p. 206, fn. 1 (he argues that the wage of a day-labourer at this time was 4 obols, the prize of an oracle at Mallus 2 obols). Not much: Jones: *Concept*, p. 218. See also Victor: *Alexander*, pp. 144–148. He suggests that 2 obols were the usual prize in Asia Minor.
89 Müller: Lukian, Ammianus Marcellinus, pp. 118–119.
90 Szlagor: *Verflochtene Bilder*, p. 52; Chaniotis: Rituale; Miron: Alexander, pp. 156–158.
91 Alex. 16.
92 Alex. 17, 26.

a good frontman.[93] Lucian sarcastically comments on the spectators' reaction to his pseudo-sacral live sex show during his celebration of mysteries: The spectators "with brogans on their feet and breaths that smelled of garlic, shouted in response: 'Hail, Alexander!'".[94] Another factor contributing to the cult's success may have been how it provided an easy way to contact the divine sphere via incubation – a task that was left entirely to Alexander.

By treating the dichotomy between poverty and wealth as major theme in *Alexander*, Lucian reflects upon one of his central concerns: the poverty and wealth of *paideia*. In other words, the difference between *paideia* and *pseudopaideia*, fake and truth, images and reality.[95] Lucian makes it clear that the majority of the sanctuary's clients were not educated and thus easily duped: "we must excuse those men of Paphlagonia and Pontus, thick-witted, uneducated fellows that they were […] He duped the simpletons in this way from first to last".[96]

However, it is important to note that material poverty and a low social status may cause this lack of *paideia* leading to naïveté and superstition.[97] But this does not mean that Lucian generally thinks that people who cannot afford a proper education are stupid (as the case of Alexander himself shows) or that he automatically credits rich people able to pay teachers with cleverness and insight. For him, it is a question of how the values of *paideia* are internalized. Only people truly devoted to the lessons of *paideia*, ready and eager to improve themselves and to properly internalize the values of education, are able to debunk the fraud. In consequence, both servants and nobles are cheated by Alexander, the poor and the rich. The latter were even his favorite victims, as he "needed […] simpletons […] and such, he said, were the

93 Alex. 26.

94 Alex. 39.

95 Müller: Schule(n) der Lügen, pp. 27–28, 35; Petsalis-Diomidis: *Truly Beyond Borders*, pp. 55–56, 65; Gunderson: Men, pp. 479, ("Lucian builds a counter-cult in honor of learning and culture in the same gesture he lays waste to the cult of Alexander"), 482–483; Luck: Witches, p. 147. On this main theme in Lucian's œuvre see Zweimüller: *Lukian Rhetorum praeceptor*, pp. 44–45, 55, 67, 104, 108–109; Swain: Three Faces, p. 23: "Lucian is famous for assaulting […] especially those who made any claim to intellectual merit, truth, or virtue." Müller: Trügerische Bilder, pp. 188–189; Berdozzo: *Götter*, p. 194–195; Corinne Jouanno: Mythe et allégorie dans l'oeuvre de Lucien. In: *Kentron* 24 (2008), pp. 183–225, here p. 220.

96 Alex. 17, 42; Luc. Alex. 9; 20 ("drivelling idiots"), 30 ("illiterate serving-people, easily deluded"). Petsalis-Diomidis: *Truly Beyond Borders*, p. 65; Chaniotis: Old Wine, pp. 70, 75; Jones: *Culture*, p. 327. On the people's reaction to the epiphany see Dickie: Divine Epiphany.

97 Alex. 30.

Paphlagonians who lived up above Abonuteichos, who were for the most part superstitious and rich".[98]

Conclusions

Alexander or the False Prophet is concerned with Lucian's major themes: pseudo-authorities, fake leaders, bad teachers, and the damage done to their naïve followers. Situated in the context of the contemporary religious landscape with the competing oracle cults, Lucian's parody of the cultural pattern of the *theios aner* sheds light on socio-religious features of his time. The figure of Alexander, "a quack who loved humbug and bitterly hated truth"[99] and whose inner qualities were corrupted by his lack of *paideia* is another form of the usual suspects Lucian ridicules: false authorities and pseudo-intellectuals deceiving people with their theatrical *habitus*, pretending to be sages, saviors, or benefactors, while actually aiming selfishly at fame and wealth. Like Alexander, Lucian characterizes unqualified rhetoricians, philosophers, and historiographers of his time as frauds taking money for fake lessons.[100]

Different aspects of poverty lie at the core of the text. Alexander's humble origins are preventing him to find true education (*paideia*) which could have improved him. This being so, his poverty leads to his corruption when he prostitutes himself and ends up as the apprentice of a crook. However, founding the cult allows him to escape from poverty. He is successful because of the intellectual poverty of his followers.

With a Platonic-Socratic tendency, the issue of payment for *paideia* is addressed. While there is the profane necessity to make a living (Lucian will have known this himself), the text at least permits the interpretation that any payment for *paideia* was a bad idea. It attracts unqualified people who falsely pose as authorities while only aiming at wealth and fame. Perhaps Alexander would not have ended up as a fraud if his inner qualities had been brought into bloom by true *paideia*. The social damage caused by fake authorities is immense: Bad teachers produce uneducated pupils. In consequence, there are the misled frauds like Alexander who cheat naïve people and victims like the followers who believed in him, even though they belonged to the educated classes.

98 Alex. 9.

99 Alex. 25.

100 Alexander's occupation as a boy prostitute is another hint as "prostitution was a favourite trope for characterizing the rhetoric of his day and its practitioners" (Kate Gilhuly: Bronze for Gold: Subjectivity in Lucian's *Dialogues of the Courtesans*. In: *American Journal of Philology* 128 (2007), pp. 59–94, here p. 85).

Glossary

Ael. VH = Aelian: *Varia Historia*
Arr. an. = Arrian: *Anabasis Alexandrou*
Arr. Per. = Arrian: *Periplus Ponti Euxini*
Just. = Justin: *Epitome of the Philippic History of Pompeius Trogus*
LCL = Loeb Classical Library
Luc. Alex. = Lucian: *Alexandros or The False Prophet*
Luc. Phars. = Lucan: *Pharsalia*
PIR^2 = *Prosopographia Imperii Romani*
Plat. Alc. = Plato: *Alcibiades*
Plat. Phaedr. = Plato: *Phaedrus*
Plat. Symp. = Plato: *Symposium*
Plut. Alex. = Plutarch: *(Life of) Alexander*
Sen. Ep. = Seneca: *Epistles*
Sen. De Ben. = Seneca: *De Benificiis*

Educating Poor Girls

The London Missionary Society in 19th Century South India

Divya Kannan

"White" Women and "Girls" in Travancore[1]

A surge in research interest on the history of girlhood worldwide has highlighted the multiplicity and complexity of the range of experiences that constitute it. As a socially constructed category, the historical shifts in the meaning of girlhood have allowed us to understand the inherent tensions and negotiations in its formation.[2] One of the key sites where these are played out is education. Central to processes of female socialization, assimilation, and resistance, various forms of schooling have impacted girlhood experiences. Schooling, in formal and informal ways, has tended to redefine young girls' roles and statuses in their cultures and societies.

Viewed as an "easily swayed" and "malleable" social category, female children, usually ranging from five to sixteen years of age, have been the target of Western Protestant missionary activity since the early 19th century in colonial lands such as India. Female missionaries attempted to separate young girls, perceived as potential "converts," from their indigenous homes, and inculcate in them habits and values along the lines of Christian Victorian morality. By reinforcing Orientalist stereotypes about colonial "heathen" women in India, Western missionaries sought to justify their own presence as "saviors". The historiographical debate on the role of "white women" in colonial South Asia has therefore complicated the picture of the "white woman" and "her burden" by locating them in multiple roles at various points in history.[3]

1 The author is a Transnational Research Group PhD Fellow, Centre for Historical Studies, Jawaharlal Nehru University, New Delhi. I would like to thank Prof. Janaki Nair, Cyril Brandt and Suchismita Chattopadhyay for their helpful comments and suggestions. All errors are entirely mine. Travancore is located in south-western India, a former princely state under indirect British rule which merged with the regions of Cochin and Malabar in 1956 to form present day Kerala.

2 For a collection of essays on "girlhood", spanning from the 1750s up to the 20th century, see Jennifer Helgren / Colleen. A. Vasconcellos (eds): *Girlhood: A Global History*. New Jersey: Rutgers UP 2010.

3 Clare Midgley (ed.): *Gender and Imperialism*. Manchester: Manchester UP 1998.

Scholarship on gender and colonialism in India, barring a few exceptions, has focused on the lives of upper-caste, upper-class women.[4] The laboring, lower-caste, poor woman, depicted as the "Other", has often been invisibilized. Owing to illiteracy and lack of rights to spaces of public deliberation, she is assumed to have played a less significant role. However, the poor received considerable attention in the history of missions, as the European missionary movement yielded the largest number of converts from erstwhile outcaste communities. Building upon earlier scholarship on missionary interventions, my goal is to trace the contours of this missionary interaction with poor, indigenous women in colonial south India in the contested arena of education. This article focuses on the female missionaries of the London Missionary Society (henceforth, the LMS) and their educational endeavors during the 19th and early 20th centuries in the princely state of Travancore, amongst so-called lower-caste groups such as the Ezhavas, Pulayars, Pariars, Kuravers, and Shanars (now known as Nadars).[5] It enquires into the nature of educational provision for female children in missionary boarding schools. What were the consequences, including unintended ones, of a gendered education which socialized them into certain societal roles? In what ways was the ideal missionary aim of making 'useful wives and mothers' fractured? By raising these core concerns, the paper attempts to understand the ambivalent shifts in the relationship between missionaries and the poor.[6]

The LMS witnessed their largest inflow of converts from erstwhile untouchable communities in the second half of the 19th century. However, these converts were commonly portrayed as "weak Christians", incapable of becoming

4 There is a substantial literature on the 'bhadralok' woman in colonial Bengal. For instance, see Lata Mani: *Contentious Traditions: The Debate on Sati in Colonial India.* Los Angeles: University of California Press 1998; Judith E. Walsh: *Domesticity in Colonial India: What Women Learnt When Men Gave Them Advice.* Lanham: Rowman & Littlefield 2004. Also see Padma Anagol: Indian Christian Women and Indigenous Feminism, c. 1850 – c. 1920. In: Clare Midgley (ed.): *Gender and Imperialism.* Manchester: Manchester UP 1998, pp. 79–103. On the formation of gendered identities in Kerala, see Jayakumari Devika: *Engendering Individuals: The Language of Re-forming in Early Twentieth Century Keralam.* Hyderabad: Orient Longman 2007.

5 The Pulayars and Pariars were the largest groups among the slave outcastes, deprived of their rights to use public roads, schools, proper clothing and freedom of labor. The Shanars and Ezhavas, involved in the processing of coconuts and related products and agricultural labor, were considered slightly higher on the social scale but equally subjected to various forms of untouchability and indignities. The Ezhavas and Shanars also practised untouchability against the Pulayas and Pariars. See Kunjulekshmi Saradamoni: *Emergence of a Slave Caste: The Pulayas of Kerala.* New Delhi: People's Publishing House 1980.

6 Esme Cleall: *Missionary Discourses of Difference: Negotiating Otherness in the British Empire, 1840–1900.* New York: Palgrave Macmillan 2012.

"true" believers in the fullest sense.[7] This ambivalence and contradiction in the evangelical project often manifested itself in the field of schooling, the provision of which differed according to the prevalent social location of the converts.

Founded in the early decades of the 1800s, the earliest stations of foreign missionary societies in British colonies initially witnessed the presence of women as "missionary wives". From the 1900s onwards, owing to a professionalization of missionary work among women, single "lady missionaries," as they were called, began to arrive.[8] But married women workers, unpaid and largely marginalized in the official mission reporting, laid the ground for the single female missionaries' further dynamic engagement in the colonies from the 1880s onwards. Contrary to normative divisions of labor in the missionary sphere, the work of women missionaries often blurred the distinctions between "preaching" and "teaching".

Various studies have highlighted how Western women were involved in colonial expansion and construction of "Englishness," albeit in different ways.[9] However, despite sharing racial affinity with the British imperial administrators, female missionaries, with the interplay of gender and class, negotiated multiple tensions, both in the metropole and colonies. In historicizing their roles, we must be wary, as Kumari Jayawardena points out, not to reduce them simplistically to agents with good/bad intentions or as collaborator/opponents of imperialism.[10] The relationships between white and colonized women were far more nuanced than is generally assumed. As Jane Haggis asserts: "Focusing on gender to the exclusion of race or class does little to capture the nature of relations between women across the colonial divide, while white women's own historical agency is limited by her all-encompassing status as patriarchical victim."[11]

7 The lingering 'heathen-ness' of the converts erected boundaries with the missionaries. The state of 'heathenism' was seen not just as religious, but also cultural and racial.

8 Rhonda Anne Semple: *Missionary Women: Gender, Professionalism, and the Victorian Idea of Christian Mission.* Suffolk: Boydell 2003.

9 Catherine Hall: *Cultures of Empire: Colonizers in Britain and the Empire in the Nineteenth and Twentieth Centuries: A Reader.* Manchester: Manchester UP 2000. Also see ead.: *Civilising Subjects: Metropole and Colony in the English Imagination, 1830–1867.* Chicago / London: University of Chicago Press 2002; Antoinette Burton: *At the Heart of the Empire: Indians and the Colonial Encounter in Late-Victorian Britain.* Berkeley / Los Angeles: University of California Press 1998.

10 Kumari Jayawardena: *The White Woman's Other Burden: Western Women and South Asia during British Rule.* New York: Routledge 1995.

11 Jane Haggis: White Women and Colonialism: Towards a Non-Recuperative History. In: Midgley (ed.): *Gender and Imperialism*, pp. 45–75.

Western female missionaries battled gender-differentiated roles within their churches while simultaneously portraying themselves as the morally superior face of the different "civilizing" missions amongst colonial populations.[12] But these did not constitute the two definite ends of the spectrum. Various white women in South Asia involved themselves in shaping local societies in different capacities, including as teachers, doctors, reformers, socialists, and trade unionists. Their work, as Kumari Jayawardena argues in the context of colonial Sri Lanka, also contributed in varying degrees to the spread of strands of feminist thought.[13] But middle-class British feminism often functioned within an imperial context, with missionary women's work assuming a highly ideological and political character, belying the oft-quoted assumption that they were simply the "softer, evangelical" faces of the Empire.

However, the presence of women workers in Travancore did not result in any substantial alteration in the mission hierarchy. Male missionaries continued to dominate as the supervisors and heads of every mission establishment and congregation. The proselytization agenda pursued amongst the indigenous was paternalistic in nature, trying to bring the converts under the leadership and authority of the missionary male. The latter headed the large number of boys schools, medical dispensaries, official mission committees and were mainly responsible for handling correspondence with LMS headquarters in London. The chief educational institution of the LMS, the college at Nagercoil, was managed by the male missionaries. They also oversaw the running of the Society's printing press, textbook, and tract production and corresponded with the Travancore administration and British authorities on a range of affairs. Yet, the management of girls' schools, zenana (literally "of the women") work, and the establishment of small-scale lace industry by the female missionaries brought women's work among women to prominence. Most male missionaries at the stations considered it to be an essential component of their work, although they undertook itinerancy, pastoral activities, and official management of the missions' various establishments. The progress in girls' schools, particularly boarding schools, was keenly followed to monitor the development of the indigenous woman against the norms laid down by the missions' Victorian ethos. Male missionaries also performed the role of inspectors of the LMS schools and regularly examined the boarding school girl pupils on Scripture and related subjects.

12 Harald Fischer-Tine / Michael Mann (eds): *Colonialism as Civilizing Mission: Cultural Ideology in British India.* London: Anthem 2004.

13 Jayawardena: *The White Woman's Other Burden*, pp. 1–27.

LMS Women's Work among Women

Feminist interpretations of imperial history have highlighted the ironies, contradictions, and challenges inherent in the missionary project, at home and abroad. On the one hand, new questions have been thrown up concerning the nature of struggles waged by women in Europe at the turn of the century and the global shifts that allowed them to move out of their homes. On the other, the changes induced in colonies through mission work and their relationship with local material cultures are also beginning to be explored.[14] What the female missionaries perceived as "reform" did not necessarily mean the same for women in the colonies.

Until 1875, women were not recruited formally by the LMS and were only sent out with their missionary husbands. In the colonies, they straddled different worlds. Missionary women tried to conduct themselves in a manner representative of English ideals of domesticity and Christian femininity. They constantly endeavored to live up to the image of the efficient "companion" and "help-meet" to their husbands, while assuming the role of quasi-mothers to colonial orphans and school pupils.[15] At the same time, their work went beyond merely teaching girls to become "better wives and mothers" and was intertwined with inculcating in them a sense of professionalism, as exemplified in the case of Bible-women.[16] Given the reality of oppressive caste relations, they were also engaged in documenting traditional practices and political changes in Travancore and alerting their supporters back home about them.

In the 19th century, despite the differences in class and race, sex was predominantly portrayed as linking women across the British Empire. Women entering missionary work were held responsible for the alleviation of their colonial "sisters" living in degraded conditions. A general consensus prevailed on the "helpless, unenlightened and secluded" condition of women in India, stripped of any agency in determining her life choices and circumstances. This depiction of the Hindu/heathen female was used to justify entry of the "superior" white woman into the colony. But the category of the colonized female

14 Elizabeth Prevost: Assessing Women, Gender, and Empire in Britain's Nineteenth-Century Protestant Missionary Movement. In: *History Compass* 7,3 (2009), pp. 765–799.

15 Clare Midgley: *Feminism and Empire: Women Activists in Imperial Britain, 1790–1865*. Oxon / New York: Routledge 2007, pp. 92–122.

16 Jane Haggis: 'Good Wives and Mothers' or 'dedicated workers'? In: Kalpana Ram / Margaret Jolly (eds): *Maternities and Modernities: Colonial and Postcolonial Experiences in Asia and the Pacific*. Cambridge: Cambridge UP 1998, pp. 81–113.

constantly shifted, with the realization that missionaries were often unwelcome in the homes of their targets: the so-called Hindu upper castes. The universality of "sisterhood", thus, couched in the language of "benevolence" and "salvation," revealed deep internal fractures, and the LMS missionaries began to look towards the poorer social groups to spread the Gospel.[17]

The earliest group of LMS female workers during the 1820s and 30s in Travancore was very limited in number, with sometimes only a single female worker at every mission station. They ran separate vernacular day schools for girls from high caste communities and Christian congregations and assisted their husbands in every aspect of administration. The LMS soon realized that their proselytization agenda would be thwarted unless they established wider contact with the Hindu/heathen women of the dominant communities. It is through these "missionary wives," who were able to gain limited access to zenana women, that the LMS men were able to initiate a dialogue with the high caste men.[18]

Though conversions were rare, zenana work continued to be at the core of women's missionary work among women. The boarding schools were established to provide adequate workers to impart literacy and Scriptures to high-caste women in their homes. But the training of low-caste girls into "true" Christians and professional workers in order to gain entry into the zenanas placed the boarding school pupils, particularly Bible-women, at a peculiar intersection of social forces.

Like their counterparts elsewhere, when the LMS set up schools in the mission districts of south Travancore, they faced prejudices surrounding female education. Travancore, ruled by an orthodox Hindu administration, under indirect British rule, practiced a stringent caste-based social hierarchy. Women across communities and classes were banned from formal schooling. The Pulayars and Pariars were slave laborers and denied many basic rights to life and freedom. The Ezhavas and Shanars, who were considered polluting but placed above the slave castes in the social scale, were predominantly involved with activities such as toddy-tapping, coconut-farming, and agricultural labor. In south Travancore, the LMS was confronted with early marriage, agrarian slavery, and religious customs, which became the biggest

17 For an excellent collection of essays that elaborate on the unequal social power between women, see Mary Taylor Huber / Nancy Lutkehaus: *Gendered Missions: Women and Men in Missionary Discourse and Practice.* Michigan: University of Michigan Press 1999.

18 Janaki Nair: Uncovering the *Zenana*: Visions of Indian Womanhood in Englishwomen's Writings, 1813–1940. In: *Journal of Women's History* 2,1 (1990), pp. 8–12.

obstacles to proselytization among women. It was difficult to regularly attract girls to school as most of them worked in the fields. Female education was also not looked upon favorably, given prevailing customs and staunch opposition from landlords, who were often unsettled by missionary interventions. In addition, the outcaste communities themselves mostly demanded education for their male children.

The solution, the missionaries argued, was a kind of education "presented as a good maternal upbringing enabling girls to take advantage of formal education, so that they can combine understanding with accomplishment, vivacity with modesty, and feeling for others with decorum."[19] With the entry of a significant number of the untouchable castes into the fold of Christianity by the 1880s, the LMS called for education to provide new opportunities for self-improvement and work. For women, these ideas were not necessarily translated into teaching them to shed their traditional roles. The key focus remained on imparting Christian virtues to make them "useful wives and mothers" and "dedicated workers," amenable towards forming Christian families and congregations. Thus, the boarding schools established at mission stations were mainly meant for orphans, fatherless, and destitute Christian girls.

These schools were located within or nearby mission premises in a bid to segregate children from their "heathen" surroundings and exert greater supervision over them. It was held that "heathen" girls, in particular, had to be taken away from their homes to be educated so as to ward off the dangerous and corrupt influences of their homes. The lingering association between the girl pupils of the boarding schools and their families troubled the missionary women. Young girls had to be constantly monitored for any sign of transgression, in order to make them "new creatures" by the end of their schooling. This emergent discourse reiterated markers of differences already prominent in the problematic binaries of Christian/heathen and British/Indian. A Christian education was to pave the way for a Christian individual, "transformed" in faith through pious actions.

The LMS had not, however, abandoned their zenana work. Instead they decided to relax their "top-down" approach towards female education. They turned towards outcaste women to instill in them notions of respectability and propriety, along the existing lines of bourgeois discourses occurring in Europe and colonies like Bengal. Yet, unlike the women of the zenanas,

19 Midgley: *Feminism and Empire*, p. 35.

whose mobility was restricted, the boarding schools also sought to train Christian girls into becoming school teachers, matrons, and nurses, all while making them prospective brides for their local mission male staff. This served an important purpose from the viewpoint of colonial labor relations. Young girls were trained for professions traditionally perceived as suiting their "innate" feminine traits of "caring" and "nurturing". But by taking them away from direct agricultural work, this training also meant confronting missionary goals. Governed by Victorian mores, the LMS missionaries sought to instill virtues of Christian femininity in poor girl pupils and erase characteristics of their agrarian, caste-ridden origins. Education would provide them with new avenues of self-expression, hitherto denied by Hinduism and Islam.

"Useful Wives and Mothers": Girls' Boarding Schools

In 1819, a year after sailing from England with her husband, Martha Mault began the first boarding school for girls at Nagercoil, with very few students and everything being provided for, "even a little fee paid to the children to induce them to come to school."[20] The children were supervised with the help of local Christian women called matrons or ayahs, who were responsible for inculcating in them "habits of neatness, cleanliness and industry."[21] Gradually, boarding schools were established in Neyoor, Quilon, and Trevandrum. However, running these schools was no easy task, because the Directors of the LMS in London provided little more than verbal appreciation. Female education, though hailed as crucial to the missionary organization, was not wholly encouraged as a full-fledged endeavor worthy of official funding. The female missionaries, nevertheless, went ahead and drew upon the contemporary philanthropic and emergent women's movements in Britain to raise funds. They also rendered personal service, mostly unpaid, until professional women workers came along in subsequent decades.

Frequent appeals were made to "Ladies Associations or Committees," linked to various denominational churches in Britain and other voluntary societies.[22] Individual monetary subscriptions, toys, clothes and sewing materials were received, and the pupils in the boarding schools were named after their

20 Isaac Henry Hacker: *A Hundred Years in Travancore*. London: London Missionary Society 1908, p. 84.

21 Ibid., p. 87.

22 The LMS Ladies Committee was formed in 1875, but no woman was appointed to the Board of Directors of the Society.

benefactors. The missionary impulse, a constituent of imperial reform, resonated with the British public.[23] In 1820, this circular-cum-appeal appeared in the Society's main journal, *The Evangelical Magazine and Missionary Chronicle*:

> Here is a whole Empire, comprising so many millions of females, in which a single school for girls has not existed for thousands of years. The females have never seen books, except in the hands of men, and have no knowledge of any one of the mental employments […] in a civilized country. Their fingers have never touched a needle, a pair of scissors, a book, or a pen and they are entirely excluded from all intellectual intercourse with the other sex.
> […] in these circumstances, to whom shall the appeal be made? Is it not manifest that the ladies in Britain are the *natural* guardians of these unhappy widows and orphans in British India? Is it possible that our fair country women, ladies of rank, of influence, of the most refined sensibility, the patrons of every charity, of all that is distinguished and benevolent in our country can, after knowing the facts in this circular, continue unmoved by the cries issuing from these fires and from the thousands of orphans which surround them, witnessing the progress of these flames, which are devouring the living mother and consuming her frame to ashes![24]

Good Christian converts were expected to send their daughters to school to learn to read and understand the word of God better. Premised on this faith, they would be the recipients and conveyors of a particular knowledge, a "knowledge" which was heavily circumscribed within the parameters of religiosity sought to be exhibited in familial and communal duties.[25]

A central feature of boarding school education was the amount of physical labor the pupils were made to carry out on a daily basis. The Matron, who was also a quasi-maternal figure like the lady missionary, was crucial in ensuring the implementation of the mission timetable. Education in the boarding schools, centered mainly on Biblical extracts, also occurred outside the confines of the class room. The girls' curriculum was not purely literary in character, but meant to visibly mold their personal habits and routines in a physical manner. Thus, the schools became sites for introducing new notions of "work" and "leisure" by reordering pupils' use of time and space.[26] Elaborate timetables

23 Frank Prochaska: *Women and Philanthropy in Nineteenth-century England.* Oxford: Oxford UP 1980. The LMS established a Ladies Committee for recruiting female missionaries formally in 1875.

24 This circular was titled: Address to British Ladies on Female Education in India. In: *Evangelical Magazine and Missionary Chronicle* (EMMC) 28 (1820), pp. 439–440, here p. 439, emphasis in the original.

25 Esme Cleall: *Missionary Discourses of Difference: Negotiating Otherness in the British Empire, 1840–1900.* Basingstoke: Palgrave Macmillan 2012.

26 For a similar discussion on boarding schools run by the Danish Missionary Society in colonial South India, see Karen Vallagarda: Adam's Escape: Children and the Discordant Nature of Colonial Conversions. In: *Childhood* 18,3 (2011), pp. 298–315.

were prepared, with time apportioned precisely among various activities. This division of time into specific activities was to teach them to be "productive" and conform to subjectivities deemed "natural" to them.[27]

The LMS did not overturn Travancorean customs entirely and indeed partly accommodated them. A description of a day in the Neyoor Girls' Boarding School will help illustrate this point further. The pupils lived with the Matron in the school compound, taught by a male headmaster trained at the Nagercoil Seminary. The children slept together in one room with coconut fiber mats on the floor. "They rise at six," wrote Mrs. Baylis to her juvenile British readers, "when they sing a hymn, and the Matron prays with them. After washing and arranging their simple toilet, it is seven o' clock when the gong is struck, and they collect in the school room for their first lessons."[28] The children attended four classes a day and were taught reading, writing, arithmetic, geography, Old and New Testaments, Malayalam or Tamil grammar, elements of natural science, ancient history, histories of India and England, singing, and lace-making. Their dining patterns were also regulated. Each girl had a brass or earthen vessel for food. "At eight o' clock, they have their first meal which consists of rice and mullaguthanni (pepper water, kind of liquid curry). From nine to twelve, they have lessons and then they have their mid-day meal which is canjee, or boiled rice…"[29]

After the mid-day meal, the children resumed their lessons from one to two o'clock. The younger ones were taught to spin cotton by the Matron until four o'clock, when school hours were over. However, the elder girls assembled at the Missionary bungalow verandah from two to five o'clock where they were taught lace-making or embroidery by the European lady missionary. Adult women workers associated with the LMS' lace industry also brought their work to be inspected.

The elder girls took turns, two at a time, to help prepare the food each day. At five o'clock, they collected firewood, drew water, and helped to beat the husk from the paddy, a task known to be strenuous. Afterwards, they were allowed to play what Mrs. Baylis calls "their curious games." The evening meal of rice and curry (usually sheep or goat) was served at seven o'clock, and the children went to sleep after prayers.[30]

27 Cleall: *Missionary Discourses of Difference*, p. 75

28 Mrs. Baylis: A Day in a Boarding School in Travancore-Neyoor. In: *Juvenile Missionary Magazine and Annual* 31 (1874), pp. 190–191, here p. 190.

29 Ibid.

30 Baylis: A Day in a Boarding School in Travancore-Neyoor, p. 191.

This ordering of the girls' daily routines was perceived as necessary to mold them into efficient women who would do the same after leaving school. The destitute and orphaned pupils were to become "model" Christians, upon whom the foundations of a new family and home rested. Their "character" formation would be determined by the level of devotion and single-minded attention to the well-being of their future families and, by extension, congregations. As Mrs. Hacker wrote of the girls in Neyoor in the 1880s, "one can make out the difference between the sharp eye and intelligent face of the educated Christian woman and the leaden expression of the Hindu woman on whom no ray of light has visited."[31] The Christian women of Travancore would become everything that their non-Christian neighbors were not: educated, devout, disciplined, industrious, and civilized. These sentiments, set in binary opposition to each other and reflective of the missionary discourses of difference, echoed in the work of the LMS throughout the century. As Catherine Hall argues, this posited difference between Christian and "heathen" women, relayed to audiences back home, was central to the construction of "Empire" and "Englishness."[32] In reality, conversions through the boarding schools tended to be few and far between, but the women constantly reiterated upon its wider influence to supporters at home. Some of the pupils, they claimed, were unable to pronounce their new-found belief openly because of lingering societal pressures and fear, although they had seemingly internalized many Christian habits.

Annual prize-giving ceremonies were held to reward pupils with the best conduct. Similarly, in the day schools, prizes were given to those with highest attendance. In many cases, the winner was chosen by the children themselves, which the missionaries argued was a lesson in self-improvement and mutual checks.[33] A Christian education culminating in conversion was depicted as having transformed converts into "cleaner and better" beings. At a time when poor girls were denied schooling opportunities, the LMS provided an avenue for acquiring it, allowing women to later work in various capacities in the local community. Yet, there were unintended consequences, as the schools failed to produce converts as originally envisaged.[34]

31 Isaac Henry Hacker: *Report of the Neyoor Mission District, South Travancore*. Travancore: Travancore District Committee 1886, p. 24.

32 Catherine Hall: *Civilising Subjects*. Cambridge: Polity 2002.

33 Mrs. Duthie: *Report of the Nagercoil Mission District, South Travancore*. London: London Missionary Society 1886, p. 40.

34 For a similar discussion on boarding schools of the Church Missionary Society in Palestine,

Christian Femininity: Challenges and Anxieties

The portrayal of female behavior as prone to "pettiness" and "transgressions" was part of a dominant nineteenth-century racial discourse that viewed women (in general) and non-European people (in particular) as intellectually and morally inferior and susceptible to varying temptations, which was reflected in their work.[35]

> Being without education, moral training, or real knowledge of the world, many women spend much time in gossiping with their friends on the most frivolous and profitless topics – dress and ornaments which are their chief delight; their husbands and neighbours and scandal of the village, stories of devils, tigers and so forth.[36]

Missionary writings depicted Travancorean women as idling away their time in trivial conversations and harboring superstitions. Convert women were perceived as the bearers of the Christian faith and held responsible for its dissemination within the family. They held a lack of proper knowledge prevented the women from leading rational lives. The LMS frowned upon the latter's daily routines and activities as a mark of their backwardness.

In the boarding schools, a constant monitoring of the young girls also required keeping a strict check on their mobility, and any hint of "deviance" was not tolerated. Periods of sickness, festivals, and holidays were looked upon with disapproval, suspicions looming large over the "moral" standards of those children returning from home. The Matron or Ayah kept an eye on the children outside of formal school hours, while the woman missionary in charge held overall supervisory authority.

> We have gained a greater insight into the character and habits of the Malayali converts. The women do not appear to be kept as secluded as among the Tamil people and they remain longer unmarried. This, in a country like India, leads to great evils. It is difficult to know how to act in cases where young women have been led astray, but we feel that to let them alone without help is to allow them to go on from bad to worse [...] I mention this here as our kind subscribers will learn by it how great a blessing a boarding school is, and how essential it is to elevate the moral tone of these poor people who scarcely think that a sin which we should blush to speak of.[37]

see Nancy Stockdale: *Colonial Encounters among English and Palestinian Women, 1800–1948.* Gainesville: UP of Florida 2007.

35 Kavita Philip: *Civilising Natures: Race, Resources and Modernity in Colonial South India.* New Jersey: Rutgers UP 2004.

36 Samuel Mateer: *Native Life in Travancore.* London: W. H. Allen 1838, p. 208.

37 Report from Quilon. In: *Annual Report of the LMS Travancore District Committee.* London: London Missionary Society 1868.

The mission sought to reconstitute the domain of morality for indigenous females through the schools.

They tried to impart Victorian norms of conduct and appearance to be followed in social intercourse. These attempts paralleled larger developments in the LMS churches. What should be done about the converts' previous marriage customs? What laws govern inheritance? Could Christians participate in festivals with families who did not convert? Esme Cleall argues that these and many more questions confronted the mission, which "in attempting to answer them erected boundaries to define it."[38] However, an exploration of these questions is beyond the scope of this paper. Anxieties prevailed, with many converts continuing to follow traditional marriage customs. Polygamy was practiced in some of the lower caste communities at the time, deeply unsettling the Church's regulations governing marriage and family life. Non-monogamous practices troubled European missionaries in other colonial regions as well, and the LMS tried to impose a broad, uniform policy. The LMS in south Travancore forbade early marriages, polygamy, and divorce, the latter often causing chagrin for families whose members had not all converted. It also prevented women from leaving their partners so easily. In 1885, problems reportedly arose among the Ezhava congregation in Quilon, where the church had insisted on Christian marriage, not easily dissolvable by the will of one party.[39]

Yet, the prevalence of agrarian slavery in Travancore remained a major obstacle in the educational activities of poor female children. The Pulaya and Pariar children were tied to their mothers' landlords and put to work from a young age. Although their motives were ridden with proselytization, by confronting landlords, the LMS female missionaries participated in a nascent discourse on the rights of lower castes to basic education, among other civil rights. The primary emphasis on conversion often took a back seat as the missionaries realized that socio-political conditions were not favorable. In 1830, Martha Mault wrote to the Foreign Secretary of the LMS, saying:

> A girl in this school had become big enough to work in her master's field, he therefore came to make his claim on her. I asked him if it would not be well for her to learn to read; whether he should not allow her to do so? He replied, it may be well for you to instruct her, as you will get a better place in heaven thereby; but it is enough for me if my bullocks and slaves do the work required in the fields.[40]

38 Cleall: *Missionary Discourses of Difference*, p. 55.

39 Knowles: *Report of Quilon Mission*. London: London Missionary Society 1885, p. 13.

40 Ibid.

She stated her concerns further:

> The owner feels himself under no obligation to provide for his slaves any longer than it is convenient to employ them; hence he calls them to work during seed time and harvest, and then dismisses them to gain for themselves a scanty and uncertain pittance in the best way they can, till the returning season.[41]

The LMS held that individuals had to enjoy a state of personal freedom in order to better receive Biblical knowledge. This would allow them to recognize the existence of sin in their everyday lives and adopt practices that would strengthen their faith. A lack of freedom for the girl pupils hampered the missionary agenda of imparting sound Christian instruction. Freedom also allowed believers to engage in productive and dutiful work, the highlights of a Protestant work ethic. The female missionaries attempted to resolve this problem by utilizing girls' labor, with the intention of making it advantageous to the mission, as well as for the children themselves. "About one third of the girls in our schools are slaves; and as the children of slaves here are always the property of the mother's master, we have formed the resolution that each girl, by her own industry, shall purchase her freedom before she leaves the school."[42]

The rhetoric of self-improvement loomed large over the mission's relationship with indigenous colonial populations, particularly poor, outcaste converts. Equipping the latter to radically protest or break away from traditional societal structures was not envisaged, although the missionaries found themselves deeply implicated in questions of rights and social assertion with their deepening engagement with the poor. Conversion to Christianity did not result in an automatic discarding of caste position and recognition of basic rights, and most converts continued to be denied the right to education, temple entry and use of public roads. The LMS missionaries reluctantly intervened in the subaltern movement for civil rights, but realizing the adverse impact of caste on their own agenda, eventually took up the cause vigorously.

Throughout the 19th century, Travancore was ravaged by a number of famines and cholera epidemics. With growing numbers of people seeking help and a decline in external funding, the LMS in Travancore found its finances under pressure. By the 1890s, a small fee was being levied to cover basic expenses for the pupils in the boarding schools. The parents paid between

41 Letter from Mrs.Mault to the Foreign Secretary (For. Secy), dated Nagercoil, 2nd June, 1830. In: *EVMM New Series* 8 (1830), pp. 540–544, here p. 540.

42 Letter from Mrs.Mault to the For.Secy. In: *EVMM New Series* 9 (1831), p. 539.

a quarter of a rupee and one rupee every month or accordingly, as monthly incomes ranged from five to fifteen rupees.[43] It cost up to three pounds a year to maintain each child.[44] Some of the parents in the congregations were too poor to pay anything, while those working with the mission paid only a small amount. With the waning of public support for foreign missions, the donations from Britain often fluctuated. As a result, many children were refused admission.

During such crises, an assured supply of food was also an incentive for many girls to remain in school. It was reported that rice, fish, and vegetables were provided in the LMS boarding institutions, with mutton once a week.[45] The missionaries also claimed that they observed hygiene standards in their establishments. This maintenance paid off when, by the end of 1870s, the number of casualties from the cholera epidemic was minimal in the schools.[46] The girls' perceptions of missionary efforts cannot be adequately assessed, but reports reveal some instances of what it meant for the pupils to attend the boarding schools. The missionaries sometimes tended to view this with disapproval, as they were suspicious of the girls' genuine desire to imbibe Christian tenets. Mrs. Wilkinson at Santhapooram notes:

> We desire, however, that the people should allow the children to enter the school to obtain knowledge, not food. When I have asked a child what message will you send to your kind supporters, the reply has often been, "Please tell them I thank them for the food they provide for me", Emma Tattersfield said, "please tell them I am much obliged for their kindness and though I shall never see them on earth, I pray God […] may meet them in heaven."[47]

The discourse of femininity, in the colonial context, placed physical labor at the center of missionary education, particularly in orphanages and boarding schools. Schooling for young girls emphasized their ability to perform physical tasks within the limits of "respectable" femininity. British Protestant missionaries, in order to intervene in the nature of work followed by women, introduced sewing, lace, and embroidery work in the boarding schools. Considered "feminine," "disciplined," "domestic," and appropriate for women to

43 Report about the Girls Boarding School at Parachaley. In: *Report of the LMS Directors*. London: Missionary Society 1892, p. 153.

44 Ibid.

45 The LMS Reports of Directors from the 1870s to 1880s mention this repeatedly.

46 The Reports of the Directors of LMS during this period indicate that the better living conditions in the schools had helped to reduce casualties.

47 Report from Santhapooram. In: *LMS Travancore District Committee*. Nagercoil: London Mission Press 1862, p. 56.

offer a way of fending for themselves, missionary women taught the children sewing skills. Raw materials for the lacework were brought from Britain, and adult female converts and senior girl pupils organized into a small-scale LMS lace industry which grew considerably over time.

Martha Mault is credited with introducing lacework in her Nagercoil boarding school in 1820, and Ann Baylis-Thomson is credited with introducing embroidery at Neyoor in 1825. However, alongside the obvious economic benefits, the missionaries laid strong claim to religious and moral ones. Activities such as sewing clothes for poor Christians and mission staff and contributing a part of their earnings to a common savings fund were directed towards instilling values of piety, austerity, and frugality. The true Christian woman was to be characterized by her values of sacrifice and self-denial.

From the 1850s onwards, the schools were in great debt and the supply of lace often exceeded demand. The cholera epidemic had killed a significant number of people in the local congregations and the missionaries wrote desperately back home asking for monetary and other donations. The deaths had made many children orphans overnight, and attendance in day schools and boarding schools reduced drastically. The responses were not always enthusiastic, and the crisis continued into the 1880s. During times of debt and disease, the schools normally shut down for a while or many of the younger girls were sent back home for an extended vacation. A rise in food and clothing prices limited the school funds, and the missionaries had to send many of the younger girls home for an extended period of time.

The Feminine Stitch

The boarding school functioned as an institution for imparting homogenizing habits, considered respectable and decent. Since evangelism's universal appeal, in principle, did not believe in caste distinctions, these were attempts to erase visible differences inscribed on the body. But erasure was followed by re-inscribing new features on the body of the convert. The missionary intervention in indigenous material cultures was to impress upon them the former's superiority. As Jean and John Comaroff have shown, every aspect of the converts' domestic and social life was meticulously observed so it could be "corrected."[48]

48 On the missionary interventions in local material cultures, see Jean Comaroff / John Comaroff: *Revelation and Revolution*, vol. 1: Christianity, Colonialism, and Consciousness in South Africa. Chicago: University of Chicago Press 1991.

In the schools, this also enabled the teachers and managers to punish any "deviant" behavior. These methods of standardizing appearances and conduct were implemented to a considerable extent by the provision of uniforms. But this rarely did anything to ease the social distinctions between the missionaries and pupils themselves, as racial differences were strongly upheld.[49] Habits of neatness such as combing one's hair, bathing, and wearing clean clothes were greatly valued, and the girls were regularly inspected.[50] Travancore was deemed lacking in purity, both moral and otherwise, and the missionaries attributed it to the ignorance of the women, whose seclusion and illiteracy prevented them from becoming proper "caretakers." The mission desired that their pupils adopt new objects and new materials to shape their new selves.

The sewing of blouses and instruction regarding modesty brought the female missionaries into the domain of material indigenous cultures, particularly with regard to clothing. In Travancore, caste inscribed itself on the body, which was also the key site for "refashioning the individual."[51] Outcaste women were forbidden from wearing a breast cloth, and neither males nor females could wear anything below the knee. Those who violated the norms were often subject to severe punishment. These ensuing caste norms conflicted with missionary notions of modesty. The Shanar community, particularly the Christian converts, driven by social aspirations, emerging political consciousness, and educational advancement found themselves at the heart of a struggle to gain the right for their women to wear the breast cloth.

The Shanar breast cloth controversy, as it is popularly known, involved longstanding conflicts with the upper caste Brahmin and Nair communities.[52] The resistance occurred over a period of time, with violent attacks on Shanars during 1828–1829 and later, in the 1850s. Culminating in the right to cover the breasts, the struggle marked a spectacular moment in the region's history

49 Report from Nagercoil. In: *LMS Travancore District Committee*. Nagercoil: London Mission Press 1860.

50 In December 1840, a missionary who inspected the Girls Boarding School at Nagercoil observed: "I was delighted with the clean, neat appearance and behaviour of the children; with the intelligence they generally displayed; and especially the readiness and propriety with which most of them replied to questions on the scriptures and various religious subjects." (Quoted in R.N. Yesudas: *The History of LMS in Travancore 1806–1908*. Trivandrum: Kerala Historical Society 1980, p. 137).

51 Jayakumari Devika, E*n-gendering Individuals*. New Delhi: Orient Black Swan 2005.

52 For more details on the controversy, see Robert L. Hardgrave: *The Nadars of Tamilnad: The Political Culture of a Community in Change*. California: University of California Press 1969, pp. 59–63.

and civil rights discourse. The missionaries petitioned primarily on behalf of their Christian women, arguing that their converts should not be subject to caste regulations and judicial action should be taken against perpetrators of violence.

The wives of missionaries encouraged adult female converts and boarding school pupils to adopt a cotton garment in the form of a jacket or loose spencer, different in design from that worn by upper caste women. This was approved by the reigning sovereign of Travancore in 1874.[53] In the boarding schools, the girls were taught to sew them. However, the wearing of jackets was fraught with tension, and as Eliza Kent argues, not passively accepted by the local Christian community, who wanted to wear the upper cloth similar to high caste women in order to gain respectability.[54] The introduction of the blouse did not quickly displace traditional hierarchies.

For the LMS, the jackets/blouses occupied an ambiguous presence in the entire discourse on decency and civilization. The blouse set the boarding school girl apart in appearance. It was likened to ushering in winds of change:

> [S]everal who have left the school also continue to make jackets [...] for themselves and others, and thus an easy way of supplying those who need jackets has been opened. What decency, what respectability, what Christian like graces accrue by the wearing of jackets!! It is a great blessing, and a great improvement in our former habits.[55]

But the wearing of the Christian jacket reinforced differences between Christian converts and upper-castes. A new faith did not allow Shanar Christians, in particular, to climb up the social ladder as easily as they had wished.

Conclusion

The missionaries hoped the children would, as a result of their education, look towards Christianity and join the global missionary cause. The provision of a gendered education remained at the heart of this hybrid discourse and tended to be immensely contested. For the poor and often orphaned girls in the boarding schools of Travancore, missionary education provided

53 *LMS Report of the Directors*, October 1859, p. 247.

54 Eliza Kent: Books and Bodices: Material Culture and Protestant Missions in Colonial South India. In: Gareth Griffiths / Jamie S. Scott (eds): *Messages: Materiality, Textuality, Missions.* St. Martin's: Macmillan 2005, pp. 67–87.

55 Report from Parachaley. In: *LMS Travancore District Committee.* Nagercoil: London Mission Press 1863, p. 25.

opportunities for acquiring literacy, allowing them to participate, albeit in limited ways, in the forging of community identities. But with waning public interest in foreign missions at the turn of the century, the project remained fractured. Enlightenment values of reason and progress, which they sought to transplant to the colonies, revealed that the trajectories of modernity were not singular but various.

Education, fundamental to the dogged conversion-oriented campaigns, was also perceived as a way to alleviate poverty and better the condition of the Christian congregations. In the case of the slave girls, it opened up a small avenue to gaining freedom from bonded labor. However, their school curriculum was largely embedded within a framework of "domestication," reminiscent of Victorian attitudes towards the poor, working classes. The LMS women missionaries ran these schools, hoping to instill in Travancorean girls the supposedly superior ideals of Christian femininity by making them more servile and obedient. This instruction was intertwined with a language of race and class in the nineteenth century. While the schools did not attract girls in large numbers, it nevertheless made advances into their lives, affecting their patterns of socialization. Imparting the basic skills of reading, writing, arithmetic, and other subjects alongside the teaching of Christian scriptures meant children spent subsequent decades constantly negotiating between the demands of a "Christian" and "secular" education. These negotiations were also based on the social inequalities they faced in the state of Travancore: an experience of girlhood laden with anxiety, uncertainty, and ambiguity.

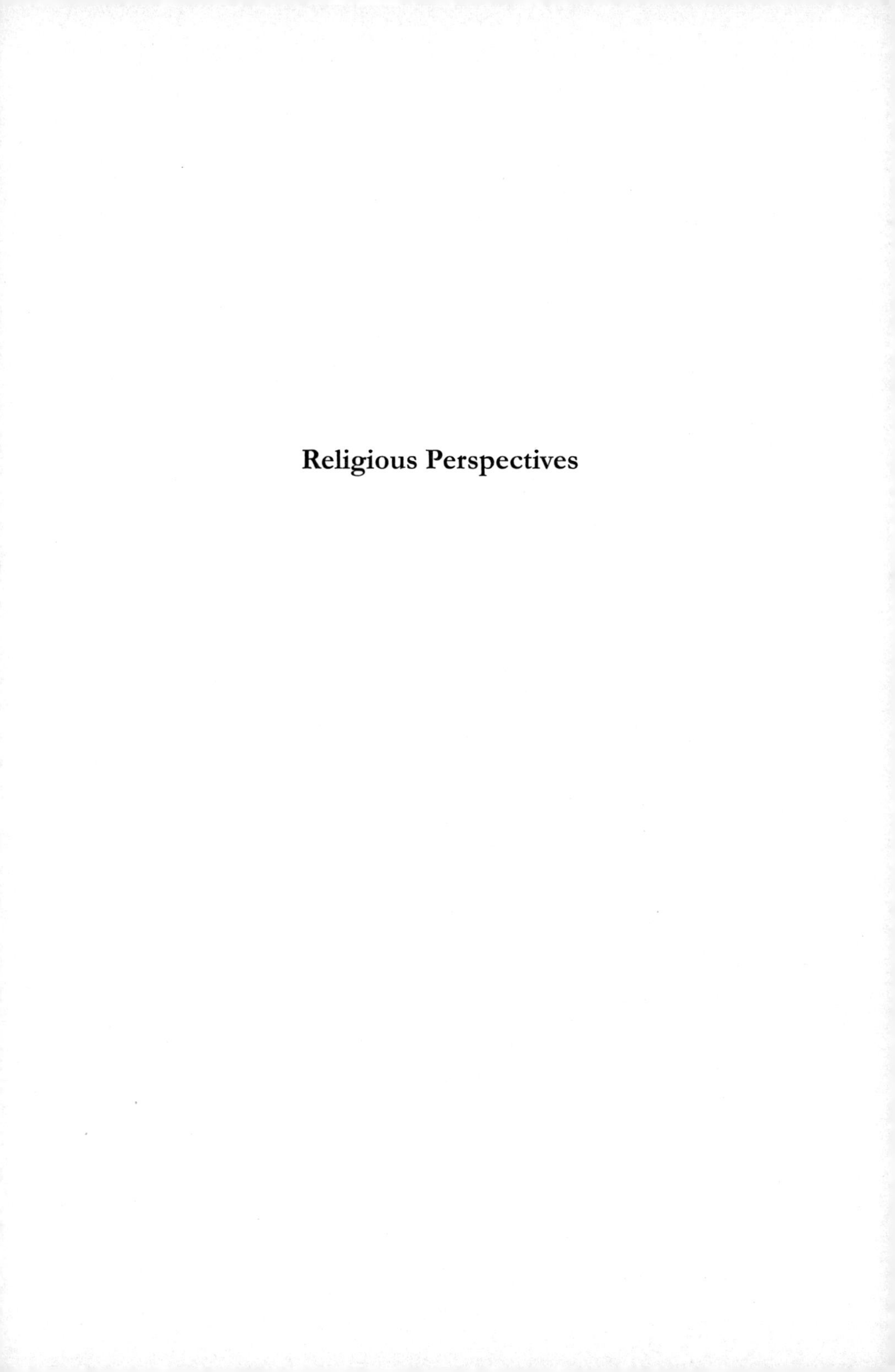

Religious Perspectives

Money to Burn

Performance of Excess and Deficit in Chinese Popular Religious Practices in Contemporary Singapore

Alvin Lim

Introduction

Local Chinese communities in Singapore burn joss paper and paper hell notes as offerings to spirits during the month of the Hungry Ghosts' Festival[1] and Qing Ming Festival.[2] This ritual can possibly be connected to the practice of issuing paper currency by fiat in the Song dynasty. It is an essential component of ancestral worship and is often publicly performed. The ritual of burning hell notes is an expression of the locals' belief that spirits have a place to go to after death. They also believe that the burned paper hell notes can be used by their ancestors and deceased family members in the afterlife. Richard Von Glahn shows how paper currency is itself a representation and a test of faith when he writes, "[p]aper money, since it clearly lacked intrinsic value, provided the most severe test of the cartalists' faith in the power of the ruler to determine the value of money by fiat."[3] The 'power of the ruler' in the case of spiritual money may come from the ruler of hell. The believer must have faith that when they use their Singapore dollars to purchase paper hell notes, the supposed tender is legitimatized by the ruler of hell (*Yan Luo Wang*). In most types of hell notes, this ruler is symbolized by images, text, and symbols printed on paper. The believer must also have faith that when the hell notes are burned, their ancestors and loved ones will receive them as spirit money. Of course, there are many who perform this ritual without faith – they do it simply because it is tradition, or in case it turns out to be true. However, without faith, the paper hell notes are just paper and cannot

1 It is believed that on the eighth month of the Chinese Lunar calendar, the gates of hell are opened for ghosts to return to the human realm temporarily to visit their loved ones.

2 The Qing Ming Festival, also known as Tomb Sweeping Day, is marked as a time when people tend their family graves. During those visits, spirit money is offered to the deceased.

3 Richard von Glahn: *Fountain of Fortune: Money and Monetary Policy in China, 1000–1700*. Berkeley: University of California Press 1996, p. 43.

Fig. 1: Example of a fifty million dollar hell note.

transform into something with larger significance that connects the earth and the underworld, the living and the dead.

The ritual is deeply rooted in the psyche and everyday life of local Chinese, who are mostly Daoist[4], yet many remain unaware or do not have a complete

4 The Daoist practice described here is a popular and contemporary form of religious Daoism. It is developed out of a popular understanding of Daoist thought and the seminal teachings of Laozi, Zhuangzi and other scriptures. Daoism has significantly developed to include an external expression of its philosophy such as ideas of *qi* (loosely translated as energy flow or force; the literal translation is "air," "gas" or "breath.") and the body as a microcosm of heaven and earth. Daoist scriptures also teach the paths to immortality and the alchemy of the inner body. These teachings support the notion of a divine order of immortals and gods. Thus, the

philosophical and historical understanding of the practice. Because of this, they have been quick to adapt and change the ritual, making it more pertinent and immediate in many aspects of their daily life. Many practitioners now place bets after burning paper hell notes, in the hope that their ancestors will bless them and let them win the lottery. Burning hell notes has become more than the symbolic exchange of paper notes for spirit money – its practice fuses reality, desire, and symbolism. Hence, by closely observing the performativity, economy, and organization of the ritual, its currency and the interrelationship between religion and poverty can be traced.

Analytical Perspective

> As a discipline, ritual studies portrays its object of study as divorced from, if not the precise antithesis of, written doctrine. Even those who criticize the tendency of ritual studies to "bifurcate thought and action" cannot wholly avoid the seductiveness of outlining a "language of action" quite separate from words, "without translating [them] into anything else." But the attempt to study ritual solely in the terms of "the qualities of human action," with little or no reference to the images and metaphors of the religious language that informs it, appears to me a vain pursuit [...]. We cannot think beyond the limits of our body.[5]

Stephen Bokenkamp's caution against "Western reading" or the imposition of "Western metaphorical structures on descriptions of Chinese ritual"[6] by some scholars provides the present study with its impetus. First, this study proposes understanding contemporary Daoist ritual as a translation of tradition. Translation already permeates the practice of popular Daoism. Daoism, as it is now practiced, performs a constant process of creativity and adaptability. Thus, this study examines the boundary-crossings of the ritual of burning paper as an offering to the dead and spirits. At the same time, it has a specific

performance of Daoist rituals is a manifestation and acknowledgment of those teachings. The rituals also relate to a worship of the gods of stars and constellations (such as the Ursa Major), heroes, and spirits of the natural world, such as the elements, mountains, seas, rivers, and animals. Popular Daoism, then, is an agglomeration of communal practices, folklore and religious beliefs historically developed. It is also a complex mixture of other popular religions, especially Buddhism. While the abstract Daoist philosophy is echoed in practice, it is also rooted in tradition that is constantly evolving.

5 Stephen R. Bokenkamp: Sackcloth and Ashes: Self and Family in the Tutan Zhai. In: Poul Andersen / Florian C. Reiter (eds): *Scriptures, Schools and Forms of Practice in Daoism: A Berlin Symposium.* Wiesbaden: Harrassowitz 2005, pp. 33–48, here p. 33. His quoted phrases are those of Catherine Bell: Performance. In: Mark C. Taylor (ed.): *Critical Terms for Religious Studies.* Chicago: University of Chicago Press 1998, pp. 205–224.

6 Bokenkamp: Sackcloth, p. 33.

geo-cultural context within Singapore's Chinese milieu. This context requires us to look anew at the difficulties of describing popular rituals.

Second, this study defines the act of burning spirit money as a figurative process of transformation and progression. C. Fred Blake writes that the burning of spirit money is "concerned with producing value, a thing of value, in the form of a sacrifice." To try and understand this sacrifice, he describes "the experience of consecrating – touching, handling, folding – the paper for the flames."[7] By applying Edmund Husserl's transcendental phenomenology, Blake finds "an uncanny likeness" between "phenomenological reduction, the suspension of our beliefs in the existence of the phenomena" and devotees burning paper money. For him, "they share a similar goal: both seek a 'reduction' of the mundane phenomenon (an object of concrete experience, in one case, and a tangible treasure, in the other) to a purer form, an eidetic form of essential meaning and true value, respectively."[8] However, this reduction is premised on what Blake calls "an attitude of plenitude," where the reduction or sacrifice is only possible when an excessive amount of paper is burned as an offering, sometimes at a great monetary cost. He writes,

> The custom has always been denigrated as a waste of paper, and in particular a waste of the labor it takes to make paper simply in order to burn it, to say nothing of the nonsense that rationalizes such waste. Today, opponents add the environmental detriments (air and water pollution and wildfires) that burning paper causes.[9]

Blake redefines labor by locating it within a supposed Chinese discourse, where the folding of gold and silver papers, sometimes done before burning paper, can be a body-objectification that ends up as self-sacrifice:

> This is not worldly labor that produces use values for exchange with others; this is, rather, the perfection of human life in the Chinese idiom of humaneness (*rén*) and ceremonial obligation in the form of giving (*lǐ*), or what we would say is a work of devotion and sacrifice to that which one is part of. In other words, folding these gold and silver papers reflects not only the sacrifice entailed in the feudal mode of production but also the sacrifice (of the self) that is necessary for civil order to exist, the highest ideal of Confucian learning.

According to Blake, the spirit money becomes "destined for destructive immolation" and realizes its "use value" by turning its "exchange value" and

7 C. Fred Blake: *Burning Money: The Material Spirit of the Chinese Lifeworld*. Honolulu: University of Hawai'i Press 2012, p. 4.

8 Ibid.

9 Ibid., p. 2.

"sign value" into "spiritual value."[10] Thus, a form of labor or "toil" precedes the burning and "[o]nce fit for immolation, the paper monies are restored to cosmic circulation via the fiery mediator of the visible and invisible."[11]

I would like to offer a different interpretation, one opposed to understanding the embodied practice as labor or works of devotion, and consequently Blake's later analysis of "ghost bills" as simulacra. In one particular analysis, Blake writes, "following the critical thought of Jean Baudrillard (1981), we might say that these new forms exhibit the change from the system of exchanging utilities into a system of exchanging signs and, thus, a system that no longer depends on production but instead relies on simulation."[12] However, simulacra – in the term's proper application – precede the productivist rationality of capital and are "not only a game played with signs; they imply social rapports and social power."[13] Despite the sense of theatricality and what Blake describes as "a kind of unreal real," Baudrillard describes a transparency of simulation that constructs social power and all its apparatuses that support this hegemony. This transparency is theatrical but also efficaciously persuasive.

I argue that the significance behind the burning of spirit money depends on the blurred relationship between what is believed in, what seems simulated by the paper notes, and what is materially expressed through the hand gestures and physical contact with the paper. Thus, the dichotomy of real and unreal is avoided and the focus is on the process and efficacy of the ritual instead. This stance is largely due to my observation of some practitioners choosing not to fold the spirit money prior to burning it. This mostly occurs in the more frequent burnings of spirit money by practitioners in designated burners (provided by the local authorities) on the first and fifteen day of the lunar month.

Heat, sweat and immolation still constitute the final act. The ritual of burning paper as spirit money is not a reduction, experienced through the sole task of folding, tossing, and burning. On the contrary, it is expansive and expresses a range of performatives – tradition, religion, the state, and one's own faith in an afterlife. It is what French philosopher Georges Bataille would call a form of "intimacy." For Bataille, "the introduction of labor into the world replaced

10 Ibid., p. 119.

11 Ibid.

12 Ibid., p. 169.

13 Jean Baudrillard: *Simulations*, trans. from the French by Paul Foss / Paul Patton / Philip Beitchman. New York: Semiotext(e) 1983, pp. 88–89.

Fig. 2: Burning of spirit money.

intimacy, the depth of desire and its free outbreaks, with rational progression, where what matters is no longer the truth of the present moment, but, rather, the subsequent results of operations."[14] Instead of merely examining the operations of burning paper, I consider the entire ritual as an intimate act, one that is, according to Bataille, "always a matter of detaching from the real order, from the poverty of things, and of restoring the divine order."[15]

> Sacrifice is heat, in which the intimacy of those who make the system of common works is rediscovered.[16]

By burning paper, or rather, by maintaining the sense of superabundance (of millions of dollars to burn), an individual makes a sacred communication with the divine order. He or she is interiorly freed from the perspective of production, labor, and productivity in the human world, which then gives rise to consumption. The burned offering translates him or her to the sacred world, albeit momentarily, or more specifically to the ancestral order as opposed to the individual. Hence, the individual interacts intimately with his

14 Georges Bataille: *The Accursed Share*, vol. I: Consumption, trans. from the French by Robert Hurley. New York: Zone 1991, p. 57.

15 Ibid.

16 Ibid., p. 59.

or her ancestors and this ritual enriches his or her experience with a feeling of abundance. In this worldview, burning must not be understood as a waste (of paper) or destruction (as fire is capable of) but a link that severs labor. It is hope *par excellence* and opens the tangible way to self-procured blessings, once the divine order is established. The act of burning, then, is an act of heat that both preserves the commonality (that we are all poor and must continue to labor) and "melts […] and blends [individuals] indiscriminately with their fellow beings."[17] In short, the physical act of burning joss paper connects individuals and sacred beings together, giving the individual a sense of hope and of being part of a larger community and family that extends beyond this life, no matter how unoriginal and "burlesque" Blake calls it. There is substance and meaning in the immolation and ashes; it is not simply an imitation of money in an unknown spiritual realm.

The concept of performativity is important to further the analysis. While it was the English philosopher John Langshaw Austin who introduced the term "performative," Shoshana Felman brought it into practice through writing – the act of doing things with words. For Austin and Felman, the distinction between the performative and the constative is weakened and dislocated when we "loosen up our ideas of truth and falsity."[18] To replace the former theory of speech acts, Austin introduces a more general theory with his doctrine of illocution – a speech performance examined with reference to the context of the interlocution, to the concrete and conventional discursive situation in which speech acquires, above and beyond its meaning, a certain force of utterance.

Felman summarizes the performative within a general doctrine of illocution and enunciatory forces, which Austin divides into five categories:

1. The category of verdicts (*verdictives*): speech acts that constitute the exercise of judgment (condemning, acquitting, estimating, evaluating, etc.).
2. The category of orders (*exercitives*): speech acts that constitute assertions of authority or the exercise of power (commanding, giving an order, naming, advising, pardoning, etc.).
3. The category of commitments (*commissives*): speech acts that consist in the assumption of an engagement with respect to a future action (promising, contracting, espousing, enrolling, swearing, betting, etc.).

17 Ibid.

18 Jong Langshaw Austin: *How to Do Things with Words*, 2nd ed. Cambridge: Harvard UP 1975, pp. 151–163. Cited in Shoshana Felman: *The Scandal of the Speaking Body: Don Juan with J. L. Austin, or Seduction in Two Languages*, trans. from the French by Catherine Porter. Stanford: Stanford UP 2003, p. 8.

4. The category of behaviors (*behabitives*): speech acts linked to a social posture (congratulating, apologizing, greeting, etc.).
5. The category of expositions (*expositives*): speech acts that consist in a discursive clarification (affirming, denying, questioning, asking, remarking, etc.).[19]

The context of the interlocution is extremely important in analyzing the performative act of burning spirit money. Often accompanying the act of burning, or "I burn," is the repeated utterance of *Huat!* (or *Prosper!* in the Hokkien dialect). In every instance of this utterance, the categories of the performative are blurred, and all categories are collectively encapsulated in a single word. As a verdict, *Huat* constitutes the exercise of estimating a large spiritual force (of the divine order) and a possible monetary windfall. As an order, it asserts and beseeches the authority of the spiritual being to bless the offering and gives credence to the utterance. As a commitment, it assumes a repeated engagement with several future acts – burning, betting or gambling, and future burning. As an exposition, it affirms all the above categories. In that sense, shouting *Huat* when "I burn" performs both the performative and the constative, at least to the believer, because it declares the successful act of burning paper and the reality of the act as a direct offering to spirits. Therefore, the performative context of the burning of money suggests the direct relation between the act and the desire to overcome one's own perceived sense of poverty.

While the symbolism of burning paper offerings is rooted in its philosophical tradition and understanding of the universe, the supposed truth of the act is no longer questioned. In one definition of the Daoist concept of *qi*, Richard C.Y. Lee, Alan Kam-leung Chan, and Timothy Y.H. Tsu associate the body with "the alchemist's 'furnace,' in which, through a series of prescribed steps, the essence and spirit can be enriched and purified to such an extent that the *qi* itself becomes the elixir (of immortality)."[20] The metaphor of a burning furnace illustrates the association of fire with the purification of material objects (such as paper) in order to reach a purer spiritual *qi* form[21]. However, as Blake points out in his ethnographic study, the "paper money custom is embedded in the matter-of-fact world of many Chinese."[22] In its place is the performative importance of the act. The repeated operation requires a

19 Felman: *The Scandal of the Speaking Body*, p. 9.

20 Richard C.Y. Lee / Alan Kam-leung Chan / Timothy Y.H. Tsu: *Taoism: Outlines of a Chinese Religious Tradition*. Singapore: Taoist Federation 1994, p. 124.

21 See fn. 4.

22 Blake: *Burning Money*, p. 10.

wider perspective to uncover the possible crossings of practices and symbolic forms.

The performativity of burning enacts the promise of a future wealth and simultaneously evokes the sense of perpetual poverty – there is never enough money. The paper regards numbers and multiplication as the ritual's guiding principle. Worked into the logic of the act of burning paper is the equation that all the spirit money burned can be exchanged for 'actual' money in hell. In fact, the low price of spirit money in Singapore (for example, a packet of hell notes can cost about Singapore dollars $1.20 and one can purchase 715 fifty million notes in one packet) supports this equation and eases the burden on the living. The multiplication is reversed when it comes to buying a lottery ticket. With a dollar, one can purchase a lottery ticket and have that one dollar multiplied should the winning numbers appear during the weekly draw.

Popular Practice

Before proceeding to analyze the practice in its context, the possible definitions of the practice warrant discussion. Because it is a practice shared by a large population of Chinese, it is possible to characterize it as one of the rituals of Chinese "popular religion." Blackwell Publishing's *A New Dictionary of Religions* gives one definition of "popular religion": "[s]ome scholars have defined it as rural in contrast to urban forms of religion, the religion of the peasant in contrast to that of the ruling classes."[23] But as suggested in the entry, there is no universal definition of popular religion:

> A major change in more recent writing is that this writer and others do treat the religious traditions so described as having their own integrity and justification without treating them as aberrations or departures from the 'norms' as laid down by the religious specialists [...] The current attitude within the study of religions has been summed up thus: 'The term "popular religion" [...] is easier to use than to define.'[24]

While "popular religion" seems "easier to use," the difficulty of defining it affects any interpretation of Asian religious forms. Stephen F. Teiser identifies three interpretations of "popular religion" and highlights the difficulty:

23 Popular Religion. In: John R. Hinnells: *A New Dictionary of Religions*. Blackwell 1995. http://www.blackwellreference.com/subscriber/tocnode.html?id=g9780631181392_chunk_g978063118139217_ss1-56 (accessed 22.02.2015).

24 Ibid.

> 1. The problem of defining "popular religion" is not simply a result of modern academic squabbles; it is also rooted in traditional Chinese sources. In discussing rites for the dead, Hsun-tzu (fl. 298–238 B. C.) explains that different social classes interpret sacrifices differently […] Hsun-tzu's interpretation allows an easy bifurcation of Chinese religion into two strata: the religion of the nobility and that of the lower classes.
> 2. Other scholars propose a second interpretation of "popular religion." From their perspective, the term designates what is shared by the *popolo*, people in general, across all social boundaries.
> 3. A third perspective on "popular religion" views culture not as an integrated whole or a possession shared by all, but as a process involving difference and dispute. Scholars following this approach suggest that Chinese popular religion should be understood less as an entity than as an activity or an arena of conflict.[25]

Furthermore, the difficulty of defining Chinese popular religious practices in Singapore has greatly exacerbated its unique nature. Religious practices are often a mix of expressions borrowed elsewhere and contents locally discovered. Hence, they are sometimes also described as "syncretized." Daniel Goh explains the limitations of such a definition and offers a way to describe Chinese religious practices in Singapore instead:

> On the cognitive level, to describe both modernity and Chinese religion as cultural systems, the Geertzian definition is useful in highlighting the existential character of both worldviews and the realist construction of sentiments in both. On this general level, we can distinguish the spatio-temporalities of modernity and Chinese religion as operating with different logics without specifying one as more rational than the other. On the level of practice, both differ on the symbolic performance that defines the identity of the adherent.[26]

Goh's first general definition, influenced by Clifford Geertz, provides a useful perspective of Chinese popular religion as a meeting point for world views to manifest in practice and shows there is no one essential characteristic of Chinese popular religion. At the same time, Goh recognizes the specificity of the performance of worshipping a pantheon of Chinese gods when he discusses his nuanced understanding of a believer's relation to his or her god:

> Elliot's (1955) discussion of the performance of *baishen* (拜神) is especially useful in this respect. But while Elliot separates out the two words, and describes *bai* as the embodied worshipping of an image involving the movement of clasped hands in front of the body and *shen* as the amorphous reference to anything spiritual, and uses "shenism" thus

25 Stephen F. Teiser: Popular Religion. In: *The Journal of Asian Studies* 53,2 (1995), pp. 378–395, here pp. 378–379.

26 Daniel P. S. Goh: Chinese Religion and the Challenge of Modernity in Malaysia and Singapore: Syncretism, Hybridisation and Transfiguration. In: *Asian Journal of Social Science* 37,1 (2009): Special Focus: Religion, pp. 107–137, here p. 111.

> to define Chinese spirit medium cults, I use the whole phrase to define Chinese religion. Contrary to Elliot's view, to *baishen* does not mean to "worship the gods" (1955:27), for this immediately contrasts Chinese religion as a polytheistic religion from the point of view of monotheistic religion and does not differentiate Chinese religion from other ostensibly polytheistic religions. To *baishen* is to engage one *shen*, and only one *shen*, using specific embodied practices (the moving clasped hands) at any moment in time in a communicative event, which may be an interlocution that involves the exchange of favours and offerings, that speaks thoughts and inspires ideas, that expresses sentiments and evokes feelings, or that articulates reverence and reaffirms sociality. The key significance here is that in Chinese religion *shen* is an almost-empty sign, a signifier referring to nothing else except the meaning of "the spiritual other." Practitioners can, therefore, fill the sign with selected concrete meanings, the possibilities of which are bounded by the historical discursive conditions of Chinese religion in a specific social context. It is therefore syncretic, in the sense that an alien deity or personage and the associated meanings may be imputed by practitioners into the sign when they *baishen* with the embodied performance.[27]

Goh's critique of Geertz's definition of *baishen* shows a careful and nuanced consideration of an individual's act or acts of ritualized behavior, such as the burning of joss paper. Goh's concept of "one shen" and "embodied practices" accurately describes the importance of relating to a single god[28] as an offering is presented to *shen*. The act of burning an offering is received by the single god or deceased. It must also be mentioned that "associated meanings imputed by practitioners" are extremely complex and convoluted. While some temples in Singapore might be dedicated to or house a single god (such as the popular Kwan Im Thong Hood Cho Temple, located at Waterloo Street), embodied practices performed in a temple can consist of a series of performatives that connect an individual to a hierarchy of gods. For example, when entering Kwan Im Thong Hood Cho Temple, a devotee would raise his or her joss sticks and face away from the temple. He or she would then proceed to offer the joss sticks to Tian Gong (or the Jade Emperor of Heaven), before heading inside to worship Kwan Im, the Goddess of Mercy.

Similarly, the type of spirit money burned depends on the spiritual being the money is being offered to. In general, hell notes or joss paper with a silver metallic rectangle are used by low-ranking spirits, unknown spirits, and spirits of the newly deceased. Hell notes with a gold metallic rectangle are generally given to high-ranking spirits, ancestors, and gods. It is important to note that different gold symbols and shapes indicate different recipients of the gold; not all deceased can receive gold. There appears to be a connection to an

27 Ibid., pp. 111–112.

28 Though I mentioned "god" in various instances throughout the paper, it is important to note, as Goh has pointed out, that every Chinese god has a specific name.

ancient understanding of money – as a general rule, gold is valued more than silver, and silver is valued more than cash monies.

Various anthropologists have attempted to trace the origins of spirit money and those endeavors characterize the second difficulty in defining "syncretized" and "popular" religious practices. In an early detailed study on the religious systems of China, Dutch Sinologist Jan Jakob Maria De Groot suggests that the transition of paper money as offerings to spiritual beings went as far back as the 2nd and 3rd centuries. [29] Hill Gates, citing Hou Ching-Lang, thinks otherwise, and writes that "the transition to paper spirit money took place in the twelfth century, which also saw the emergence of traditional banking institutions and the widespread use of paper currency."[30] Gates, however, doubts that "the version of the debt rituals [offering of spirit money] current in Taiwan date from the Song."[31] While the widespread use of paper spirit money may be accorded to the Song period, John L. McCreery notes that "the use of unreal analogues of money as offerings goes back much further […] to prehistoric times."[32] I have similar doubts that the burning of paper spirit money in Singapore has direct roots in 12th century China, let alone prehistoric times. Based on the literature and observations of the practice in Singapore, however, the various interpretations of the origins of spirit money and its usage express a common aspect of the ritual's performativity – the exchange of one reproduction for another and as an ongoing performance of transactions.

The Performative Exchange: Excess and Deficit

The performativity of substituting one medium for another remains the principle of the popular practice, whether that takes the form of paper, food, or objects. The "I offer" or "I burn" is significant here, because the act of offering is not a linear transaction, that is, an offering without return.

Hill Gates provides a concept for understanding the practice. She argues:

29 Jan Jakob M. De Groot: The Religious System of China. Leiden: Brill 1892–1910. Reprinted Taipei: Ch'eng-wen 1969, pp. 713–714.

30 Hou Ching-Lang: Monnaies d'Offrande et la Notion de Tresorerie dans la Religion Chinoise. Paris: Presses Universitaires de France 1975. Cited in Hill Gates: Money for the Gods. In: *Modern China* 13,3 (1987): Symposium on Hegemony and Chinese Folk Ideologies Part II, pp. 259–277, here p. 272.

31 Gates: Money for the Gods, p. 272.

32 John L McCreery: Why Don't We See Some Real Money Here? Offerings in Chinese Religion. In: *Journal of Chinese Religions* 18,1 (1990), pp. 1–24, here p. 6.

> Money is a natural symbol for both transformation and reproductive increase. As it serves as a medium for the exchange of commodities, it is easily fetishized – perceived as an active entity – a kind of reverse alchemist's stone that "transforms" one commodity into another. Itself inedible, unwearable, and perfectly artificial, money can transform itself through the act of purchase into commodities of many sorts. It represents in straightforward fashion the exchange of properties of a market economy. In addition, as Marx pointed out, in a capitalist context, money – to use the customary fetishizing language – "reproduces itself" like a living being.[33]

For Gates, the burning of spirit money "represents [...] the exchange of properties of a market economy."[34] In fact, it is not just money that can be exchanged, but paper clothes and wares (scissors, mirror, shoes, etc.) can be burned and exchanged for 'actual' clothes in the spiritual realm. More recently, paper iPhones, iPads and laptops can be burned and offered to the deceased.[35] These paper offerings may be imitations and it may seem too farfetched to even comprehend how paper can materialize as mobile phones, tablets, and laptops complete with the latest processor chips. But as Gates suggests, this exchange extends beyond the symbolic and the spiritual; it affirms the concept of a continual cycle of rewards as the debt of the deceased is paid off by the living, and the debt of the living is likewise paid off by the spirits:

> That the gods are concerned with honesty and uprightness in human transactions, and reward these with prosperity, is commonplace among small business-people and craft workers. Paying one's debts, an essential duty on earth, becomes elevated through ritual to a sacrament in heaven, an act of personal salvation.[36]

Debt, as McCreery also explains, motivates the burning of large quantities of spirit money:

> It is, however, the burning of large quantities of spirit money that makes the difference in how severely a person is punished when, having died; he once again faces the courts of Hell. This rationale explains why people burn such large amounts of spirit money at funerals, for no one ever complete succeeds in repaying his celestial debt. His descendants must pay for him.[37]

The performative act of burning spirit money is a transaction with possible value in the human world. The ritual of burning elevates the supposed copy.

33 Gates: Money for the Gods, p. 261.

34 Ibid.

35 Karen Gwee: Afterlife 'Upgrades'. Replicas of Daily Items, Vehicles Are in Demand for Qing Ming Festival. In: *The New Paper*, 03.04.2013. http://www.asiaone.com/print/News/Latest%2BNews/Singapore/Story/A1Story20130402-412947.html (accessed 27.02.2015).

36 Gates: Money for the Gods, p. 271.

37 McCreery: Why Don't We See Some Real Money Here?, p. 5.

It is thus not imitation, *per se*, but works on the logic of multiplication. When a devotee burns spirit money, a request can be made for material possession or to win a lottery. It can also be an act of thanksgiving for a windfall after the deceased has apparently blessed the devotee with a vision of winning numbers, usually in a dream. All it takes is for an individual to believe that a spiritual intervention has taken place during the process of betting in order for that individual to continue and promote the practice of burning spirit money. The fact that spirit money is cheap to buy and yet has an incredibly high value in the underworld makes it easy for the individual to pay off his or her debts (monetary and emotional) to the deceased. It also becomes a way for the individual to maintain, increase, and/or show off his or her wealth and luck. Wealthy Chinese families often spend a lot to prepare paper offerings and possessions (such as paper buildings, cars with chauffeurs, an entourage of domestic workers, etc.) for the dead during funerals and death anniversaries as an elaborate show of their status and wealth in society. All of these feed into an imagined sense of poverty and/or deficit.

Goh's argument of the intimate and personal relationship with a spirit is crucial to my analysis. By definition, a sacrifice is an offering to the gods and spirits. The *Analects*, a collection of sayings by Confucius brought together by his followers, states:

> 祭如在、祭神如神在。子曰。吾不與祭、如不祭。
>
> [When Confucius offered sacrifice to his ancestors, he felt as if his ancestral spirits were actually present. When he offered sacrifice to other spiritual beings, he felt as if they were actually present. He said, "If I do not participate in the sacrifice, it is as if I did not sacrifice at all."][38]

The speech acts of "I burn," "I offer," and "I sacrifice" effectuate the process of exchange and this exchange is a continual loop. According to Confucius, the individual participates in a communal act of burning spirit money and relates to the spirit through the embodied ritual. In a more contemporary sense, when "I burn" money is coupled with a shout of "Huat," the performative utterances establish a promise – or rather the lure of a promise – of fortune and happiness. An individual's actions are motivated or governed by the promises he or she makes to the spirit, and *vice versa*, and those actions will maintain the symbolic exchange (when successful). Such promises lure the

38 Chapter 3:12 of The Humanism of Confucius. In: *A Source Book in Chinese Philosophy,* trans. from the Chinese by Wing-Tsit Chan. Princeton: Princeton UP 1973, pp. 14–48, here p. 25.

individual to burn spirit money and also to buy (a lottery ticket and packets of hell notes), in the hope of future prosperity.
It must be said that "I burn" is not done solely for future wealth. The involvement of money is also a show of affection, love, respect, and reverence. During Chinese New Year, for example, red packets of money (*hong bao*) are given to the young and old as a sign of love and to bless the recipient. Similarly, when the living are able to offer money to their deceased loved ones, the gesture of burning spirit money is an expression of filial piety and love. In that sense, when an individual wins the lottery and pays his or her respects to the deceased, it is an acknowledgement of the deceased's act of blessing and watching over the individual.

The Burned Money: Ashes and the Afterlife

Burning, then, is a series of performatives. The performatives engage the individual in multiple ways. Beyond the individual, it is vital for the community that the ritual is performed, because it continues the narrative of the afterlife and the involvement of spirits in the affairs of people, as well as the ability of the people to continue taking care of their loved ones beyond this life. The current study analyses the burning of money in more expansive terms than the descriptions offered by Fred Blake, such as:

> The paper money custom is dramatic and colorful; waxing rhetorical, I often call it a potlatch for the spirits. As such, it is photogenic. It lends itself to visual imaging and representation, representations of representations, via mechanical reproduction, to which our modern lifeworld is hopelessly addicted.[39]

The devotee progresses the burning beyond a spiritual act and includes it as a practical mode of expression. The contemporary expression has perhaps taken a mechanical turn of reproduction and, as mentioned, multiplication. However, that is to misunderstand and equate mimicry as the *modus operandi* of Chinese devotees. Burning money is not simply "photogenic," but a solemn reminder of and comforting certainty in what lies beyond life on earth for these practitioners. The present study cannot ascertain the existence of a hell with inhabitants that are capable of making transactions with gold, silver, and cash, but the study takes into account the hybrids created by Chinese communities when they encounter disparate symbolic forms. Daniel Goh writes

39 Blake: *Burning Money*, p. 5.

about the "disfiguration and anxiety resulting from the meeting of Chinese religion and modernity" and concludes that:

> The hybrid created by prophetic innovations contains and combines the very disfigurements. Likewise, the fetish contains and exudes the very anxieties thrown up by the encounter of disparate symbolic forms. In this sense, the Chinese in Malaysia and Singapore have innovatively displaced existential disfiguration and anxiety into the hybrid and fetish, using these to deal with their everyday lives.[40]

The symbolic forms are not derived from a single source. Nor do they react to a single condition, such as having to offer money to spirits and gods. Social power is negotiated in any instance of burning money because of the sociocultural position it plays. For instance, when the ritual is carried out in public areas, the devotee is legally obliged to clean up after they have given their offerings. When burning joss papers, candles, etc., they should use burners. Town councils for housing estates provide burners (such as the one shown in Figure 2), usually during the month of the Hungry Ghosts Festival. On the website of the National Environment Agency, which is a statutory board under the Ministry of the Environment and Water Resources in Singapore, the following frequently asked questions are given to clarify the protocols of burning:

> Are people allowed to burn joss-papers and candles in public places?
>
> The public must clean up the place after they have made their offerings. When burning joss-papers, candles, etc. they should use containers. Residents in town council estates should make use of the burning pits and containers provided by the town councils.
>
> To minimise problems when burning joss-papers, candles, etc., the Government introduced the following control measures on 1 March 1998:
> - Joss sticks shall not exceed 2 metres in length and 75 mm diameter. For large joss sticks up to 2 metres in length and 75 mm in diameter, no more than six may be burnt at any one time.
> - Candles shall not exceed 600 mm in length. For large candles up to 600 mm in length, no more than two may be burnt at any one time.
> - The burning of large joss sticks and candles shall not be within 30 metres from any building.[41]

Town councils also put up posters to promote the responsible burning of joss paper and spirit money.[42] When such rules are not followed, complaints

40 Goh: Chinese Religion and the Challenge of Modernity in Malaysia and Singapore, p. 134.

41 National Environment Agency, Singapore: Frequently Asked Questions. http://www.ifaq.gov.sg/NEA/apps/fcd_faqmain.aspx#FAQ_31167 (accessed 12.02.2015).

42 One such poster can be found on the website of the Ang Mo Kio Town Council at http://www.amktc.org.sg/pub_edu-poster.aspx (accessed 12.02.2015).

can also be found on government-related websites.[43] The burners perform the state's regard of public space as state property. When fires made by devotees destroy public property (usually because they do not burn paper money in the burners but on concrete pavements or grass patches instead), they are fined and the town councils have to spend money to fix the damaged property. Cleaners are also hired to remove unused paper, burned joss sticks, and food offerings left near the burners. These periods of widespread burning around Singapore can take a toll on town councils, but the expense of cleaning up is mostly covered by the conservancy charges and arrears that residents must all pay to the town councils. Thus, in Singapore's case, the burning of spirit money appears less as a burlesque or a spectacle (in Blake's terms) than as an organized activity that has to operate within clear parameters. Though these regulations are sometimes flouted, there is an understanding that consequences are meted out to those who disobey. More importantly, the practice has to negotiate with Singapore's need for religious sensitivity, as Singapore is a renowned melting pot of races, cultures, and religious beliefs. Goh's description of disfigurements is clearly shown in the state's control of burning. Thus, the transference of capital, minimally spent in buying the cheap paper money, progresses to the level of the social. To burn "irresponsibly" is to increase the chance of paying higher conservancy charges. Burning money, then, performs more than just its spiritual meaning – it performs a societal one as well.

Conclusion

The burning of spirit money operates at several levels of performativity. On one level, it enacts the practitioners' belief that there is a spiritual realm where 'actual' money can materialize after its paper form has been burned in the human realm. On another level, it expresses the hope that one can financially excel despite one's poverty (whether real or perceived). Because burned offerings can be performed with relative ease, chance is readily bought and informs the buying of lottery tickets. Its symbolic meaning is entangled with a practical desire, embodied in the lottery, either in the form of the four-digit number draw (4D) or the six number draw (Toto).

43 Complaints can be read from a government website at https://www.reach.gov.sg/YourSay/DiscussionForum/tabid/101/Default.aspx?ssFormAction=%5B%5BssBlogThread_VIEW%5D%5D&tid=%5B%5B12727%5D%5D&mode=3 (accessed 12.02.2015).

The dreams and number combinations that the practitioners receive at temples and gravesides can motivate them to form long queues at betting stations. Once, after visiting my grandmother's tomb at Lim Chu Kang graveyard during the Qing Ming Festival, my relatives concluded their prayers to her by asking for a successful lottery draw. While this is essentially the expression of hope, offerings are inevitably linked to chance. But chance has to conform to social hegemony. The betting stations are owned by authorized sellers of lottery tickets, issued by the state-owned lottery subsidiary, Singapore Pools Limited. When transactions are made, money changes hands, spirits, and authorities.

Therefore, to speak of burning money is to inquire into the very nature of Singaporean society. It is a society that models itself on a general economy based on excess and luxury, and a widespread financial aspiration to "raise the living standard."[44] This excess and luxury, however, is also mostly purchased with debt, as Singaporeans take on loans to purchase leases for public houses built by the Housing Development Board and ten-year certificates of entitlement to drive cars on Singapore roads. When Bataille describes post-war man, he writes that "man is the most suited of all living beings to consume intensely, sumptuously, the excess energy offered up the pressure of life to conflagrations befitting the solar origins of its movement."[45] The aspiration of many practitioners is to escape debt, and this is underscored by the fact that, at the highest point of burning, its significance is still veiled. Only ashes remain, and there is no way to watch their transformation to luxury in the otherworld; one has to simply have faith that it will happen. Fire and heat, the sweat it draws from man, and the physical act of destroying useful paper is perhaps a protest against luxury and an affirmation that one can afford to inflate money and destroy it in the same gesture, as hinted at by Bataille. Burning is not a requirement of luxury.[46] Yet it gives the assertion that man is insured against the risk of having nowhere to exist, and also has the power to raise the standard of living in hell (and on earth). "I burn," then, means to be moved to perform and to be intimately involved in the act, even if it veils the significance it had to the spiritual condition. More accurately, it is because "we burn" that the practice remains a widespread and evolving phenomenon.

44 Bataille: *The Accursed Share*, p. 41.

45 Ibid., p. 37.

46 Ibid., p. 38.

Providing for the Poor, the Widow, and the Orphan

A Social and Religious Ethical Revolution in the Jewish Bible[1]

Jeremiah Unterman

Social justice in ancient Near Eastern (henceforth, ANE) societies was not identified with equality, nor was it identical with the elimination of poverty as such, since it was accepted that large sections of the population would constantly exist at subsistence level. Social justice was perceived rather as protecting the weaker levels of society from being wrongly deprived of their due: the legal, property, and economic rights to which their place within the social hierarchy entitled them.[2] Then or now, any government or society concerned with social justice needs to address the condition of its economically and socially disadvantaged elements. Such attention to this need should minimally result in a system for alleviating this condition and enabling the disadvantaged to attain enough practical support to continue to co-exist with the more fortunate members of society. A related question concerns the social standing of the disadvantaged: are they perceived as inferiors or as equals and, specifically, what are the parameters of this perception?

This paper will survey the Jewish Bible's consideration of the disadvantaged by focusing on the poor, the widow, and the orphan. It will be conclusively shown that in each category the Bible, in ethical terms, far outstrips the literature of the surrounding ANE societies.

Fifty years ago, a famous academic article on the poor, widow, and orphan in the ANE[3] argued that "The basic conception in all the literature discussed

1 This paper is adapted from a chapter in a book being written on ethical innovations in the Jewish Bible. As that book is addressed to English-speaking laypeople, the references here do not include material from other languages.

2 Raymond Westbrook: Social Justice in the Ancient Near East. In: Kaidhosrov D. Irani / Morris Silver (eds): *Social Justice in the Ancient World.* Westport, CT: Greenwood 1995, pp. 149–164, here p. 149.

3 F. Charles Fensham: Widow, Orphan, and the Poor in Ancient Near Eastern Legal and Wisdom Literature. In: *Journal of Near Eastern Studies* 21 (1962), pp. 129–139, reprinted in Frederick E. Greenspahn (ed.): *Essential Papers on Israel and the Ancient Near East.* New York: New York UP 1991, pp. 176–192.

is that the protection of the weak is the will of the god."[4] Charles Fensham further states, "This is one of the most important ethical doctrines of the Old Testament, but definitely not unique in comparison with conceptions in neighboring cultures."[5] Finally, the author concluded:

> The attitude taken against widow, orphan, and poor is to be looked at from a legal background. These people had no rights, no legal personalities, or in some cases possibly restricted rights. They were almost outlaws. Anyone could oppress them without danger that legal connections might endanger his position [...] Therefore, it was necessary to sanction their protection by direct command of the god and to make it the virtue of kings [...] in the history of the ancient Near East the compulsion was felt to protect these people [...] In the Israelite community this policy was extended through the encouragement of the high ethical religion of Yahweh to become a definite part of their religion, later to be inherited by Christians and Moslems.[6]

At no point does that author mention the fact that *only* in the Jewish Bible the concern for the poor, widow, and orphan is translated into law, along with its specific periodic obligations, as we shall see below.[7] First, I will briefly survey the relevant ANE literature.

Poverty in ANE Literature[8]

Egypt

Before it came under Greek Ptolemaic rule, Egypt's extraordinary civilization lasted some 2700 years, with its first dynasty founded in approximately 3000 B. C.[9] Its many inscriptions, monuments, pictorial depictions, and papyri

4 Fensham: Widow, Orphan, and the Poor, pp. 186–187.

5 Ibid., p. 187.

6 Ibid., pp. 188–189.

7 Since the references to the widow and orphan in both the ANE and Israel usually refer to impoverished widows and orphans (with the exception of actual ANE laws, see below), they are subsumed together here under the general designation of poverty. Further, the poor in the literature cited below refers to members of the dominant society and not resident aliens. In the Jewish Bible, resident aliens received considerable benefits and were often included together with the poor, but, to do that subject justice, this paper would have to be twice its size.

8 I have been particularly aided here by the work of Harriet K. Havice: *The Concern for the Widow and the Fatherless in the Ancient Near East: A Case Study in Old Testament Ethics.* Ph. D. dissertation, Yale University 1978, who collected more relevant information on the poor and weak in Egypt, Mesopotamia, and Ugarit than I have found anywhere else.

9 For a detailed chronology, see Kenneth A. Kitchen: Egypt, History of (Chronology). In: *Anchor Bible Dictionary*, ed. by David Noel Freedman. New York: Doubleday 1992, vol. 2, pp. 321–331, particularly pp. 327–329, and the articles following.

provide a wealth of information about Egyptian society and religion. It should be noted that no ancient Egyptian law collection exists.

Throughout much of the Egyptian kingdoms, idealized biographies and protestations of innocence (before dying) were written which attested that the authors took care of the poor: "I gave bread to the hungry, water to the thirsty, clothing to the naked" (ca. 21st cent. B.C.);[10] "I did that which men praise and with which the gods are pleased. I gave bread to the hungry and satisfied those who have nothing" (ca. 16th–15th cent. B.C.);[11] "I spoke for the widow on the day of justice" (2700–2200 B.C.); "I gave to the beggar (poor), I nourished the orphan" (Amenemhet I, ca. 21st cent. B.C.); "there was no widow whom I oppressed" (Sesostris I, ca. 21st cent. B.C.); "I was a father to the poor, one who cared for the widows" (Mentuwoser, 21st cent. B.C.).[12]

Numerous such declarations of innocence appear in the Book of the Dead (16th–15th cent. B.C.), in which the deceased addresses each of the 42 divine justices: "I have not done violence to a poor man [...] I have given bread to the hungry, water to the thirsty, clothing to the naked, and a ferry-boat to him who was marooned [...] so rescue me, you; protect me, you."[13] These set phrases (and others) only applied to the upper class in the Old Kingdom (2700–2160 B.C.). In a democratization of the netherworld, by the Middle Kingdom (end of the third millennium B.C.) the common man is recognized as having some duty of beneficence to those more needy than himself. These declarations alone seem to have some magical effect – to clear away sin even if pronounced by someone who led an immoral life. However, that the deceased aligns himself with these ethical statements implies an acceptance of these standards as willed by the gods.[14]

Governing these statements was a philosophy of reward and punishment – good acts brought good fortune; evil acts brought misfortune. In the early period, Egyptian ethics saw the connection between an act and its consequences as a natural occurrence which took place without any divine intervention. By the late period, the connection between an act and its consequences was seen as being divinely mediated. In later Egyptian thought, misfortune came to be seen as evidence of wrongdoing, while good fortune was proof of virtue. Reward and punishment in the afterlife could function as a theodicy

10 Havice: *Concern*, p. 29.
11 Ibid., p. 21.
12 Ibid., pp. 31–32.
13 Ibid., pp. 46–47.
14 Ibid., pp. 49–50.

(justification of divine behavior) to explain how an evil man could prosper in this life despite the gods' wishes. The soul of the dead would appear before a tribunal of the gods. It could be found so wicked that it would be immediately extinguished, or so virtuous that it was raised to the position of a god in union with the god Osiris.[15]

Grave inscriptions which state that the deceased "fed the hungry, watered the thirsty, and clothed the naked" afterwards request that the visitor to the grave offers bread and beer for the soul of the deceased, as the deceased is seen as in poverty and need – with an emphasis on thirst and hunger. So, funerary offerings of food and water were necessary to sustain the dead and were often placed at his tomb site. The listing of beneficent acts was designed to motivate the readers to do corresponding acts of kindness for him, that is, he is "owed" these acts as recompense for his own similar behavior. This listing, then, is not induced so much by altruism as by the wish to maintain one's own existence.[16]

The purpose of Egyptian wisdom instructions was to teach the son that to be a successful ruler he must learn the behaviors in accord with the right ordering of society, the principles of *maat* (truth/justice/right order)[17] which correspond to the divine order.[18] Examples of instructions to care for the underprivileged are: "Do justice that you may live long upon the earth. Calm the weeper, do not oppress the widow, do not oust a man from his father's property"[19] (Merikare, 21st cent. B.C.);

> Be not greedy for the property of a poor man, nor hunger for his bread […] Be not greedy after a cubit of land, nor encroach upon the boundaries of a widow […] Do not recognize a widow if you catch her in the fields [perhaps implying that the widow has some permission to glean in those fields], nor fail to be indulgent to her reply. Do not neglect a stranger (with) your oil-jar […] God desires respect for the poor more than the honoring of the exalted. (Amenemope, 13th cent. B.C.)[20]

15 Havice: *Concern*, pp. 36–40.

16 Ibid., pp. 43–44.

17 *Maat* does not only signify these virtues, but is also an Egyptian goddess, see Leon Epsztein: *Social Justice in the Ancient Near East and the People of the Bible,* trans. from the French by John Bowden. London: SCM 1986, p. 18.

18 Havice: *Concern*, pp. 52–57. The words for "teacher" and "father" are the same and the words for "student" and "son" are the same. Later (19th Dyn.) there is evidence that these became the instructions for the teaching of children.

19 R. O. Faulkner / William Kelly Simpson (eds): *The Literature of Ancient Egypt.* New Haven / London: Yale UP 1973, pp. 180–192. http://www.reshafim.org.il/ad/egypt/merikare_papyrus.htm (accessed 01.07.2015).

20 Ibid., pp. 64–67. Note that the stranger, widow and poor are combined here.

Examples of hymns and petitions or prayers that portray both gods and officials as concerned for the disadvantaged are: "free from partiality, justifying the just […] servant of the poor, father of the fatherless […] protector of the weak, […] husband of the widow, shelter of the orphan" (Intef, the royal herald, 16th–14th cent. B. C.); "Because you are the father of the fatherless, the husband of the widow […] the apron of him that is motherless […] one who destroys falsehood and brings justice into being" (Protest of the Eloquent Peasant, 20th–18th cent. B. C.); "he who hears the prayer, who comes at the voice of the poor and distressed […] you are Amon […] who comes at the voice of the poor man" (to the god Amon-Re, 18th–16th cent. B. C.); "Do (not) widows say, 'Our husband are you' and little ones 'our father and mother'? […] the poor worship your face" (Hymns to the Gods as a Single God, circa 1300 B. C.).[21]

In sum, in the Egyptian worldview one owes loyalty and obedience to one's superior, and kindness to one's inferior – the beneficence given to the inferior is reciprocated by loyalty and obedience.[22] According to their textual prominence, the Egyptian who wishes to live a virtuous life must display these characteristics: family affection – respect and love of parents, and solicitude for siblings and offspring; honesty and truthfulness in all circumstances; justice and fairness to all (the special concern of the public official); kindness and benevolence to all; loyalty and devotion (to one's superiors and gods); diligence and competence; moderation, including modesty, calm, and peacefulness.[23] Of course, one must temper these moral attitudes with the realization that they did not apply to the lives of slaves.[24]

21 Ibid., pp. 74–86.

22 Ibid., pp. 94–95.

23 Miriam Lichtheim: *Moral Values in Ancient Egypt.* Göttingen: Vandenhoeck & Ruprecht 1997, p. 87.

24 Anthony Leahy: Ethnic Diversity in Ancient Egypt. In: Jack M. Sasson (ed.): *Civilizations in the Ancient Near East*, vol. 1. New York: Scribner 1995, pp. 225–234, states: "Throughout ancient times, there was a significant substratum of foreign slaves in Egypt who were engaged on royal building projects […] The majority were the booty of war […] Many arrived in Egypt through various forms of the slave trade […] Ramsses II did not hesitate to uproot large groups of people […] People enslaved in this way are individually invisible to us; they were condemned to remain at the lowest level of society and to labor their lives away in abysmal conditions on building sites or in mines and quarries of the Eastern Desert. They are often even collectively anonymous: there is no clear trace of the Hebrews in Egyptian sources, for example" (ibid., pp. 228–229). At the same time, Leahy writes, "The capacity of Egyptian society to absorb people from a wide variety of ethnic backgrounds without prejudice was one of its characteristic features. The only requirement was a willingness to integrate. Signs of ethnic tension surface only rarely, when groups actively sought to retain their ethnic character by conspicuously adhering to un-Egyptian practices or by maintaining a high profile or physical separateness." (Ibid., p. 233).

Mesopotamia

In ancient Mesopotamian literature, concern for the disadvantaged was not as prominent as it was in Egyptian. Only infrequent mentions of the widow and orphan occur.[25] Reminiscent of the prologues and epilogues to certain law collections (see below), references to the underprivileged are found in building inscriptions which were buried from view and meant to address the gods or future kings, including: the reform of Urukagina of Lagash (24th cent. B.C.), as opposed to what happened previously, "the one in charge of the food supplies did not dare enter the garden of the indigent mother" to take the fruit, and "if the son of a poor man laid out a fish pond, the influential man did not dare take away its fish […] Urukagina made a compact with Ningirsu that a man of power must not commit an injustice against an orphan or widow"; of Sennacherib (Assyria, 8th cent. B.C.) "Guardian of the right, lover of justice […] who comes to the aid of the needy"; Sargon II (also, Assyria, 8th cent. B.C.) claims he was elected by the gods "to maintain justice and right, to give guidance to those who are not strong, not to injure the weak"[26]. Such ideas are also mentioned in hymns/petitions and incantations.[27] Similarly to Egypt, Akkadian wisdom literature (8th cent. B.C.) states that the wise man should, "The one begging for alms, honor, clothe […] this is pleasing unto the god Shamash, he rewards it with good."[28]

Of primary interest, particularly in contrast to the Jewish Bible, are references to the disadvantaged in ANE law collections. The prologue of the Ur-nammu (King of Ur) collection (ca. 2100 B.C.) states, "I did not deliver the orphan to the wealthy man; I did not deliver the widow to the mighty man; I did not deliver the man of one shekel to the man of one mina (that is, 60 shekels)." Similarly, the epilogue of the Hammurabi law collection (ca. 1750 B.C.) declares, "In order that the strong might not oppress the weak, that justice might be dealt the orphan (and) the widow, in Babylon […] I wrote my precious words on my stele […] to give justice to the oppressed." Further, Hammurabi asserts in the prologue that he was appointed by the gods "to promote the welfare of the people […] to cause justice to prevail in the land, to destroy the wicked and the evil, that the strong might not oppress

25 Havice: *Concern*, p. 101.

26 Ibid., pp. 107–111.

27 Ibid., pp. 149–163.

28 "Counsels of Wisdom," trans. by Robert H. Pfeiffer. In: James B. Pritchard (ed.): *Ancient Near Eastern Texts Relating to the Old Testament*, 2nd ed. plus supplement. Princeton: Princeton UP 1971, p. 426, lines ii, 13–16.

the weak"[29]. As is evident, the divine commission obliges the king to protect the weak from harm by the wealthier or more powerful. However, unlike Egypt, there is no mention of the king's responsibility to provide beneficence to the underprivileged.[30]

In the laws themselves, numerous statutes mention the widow (less so, the orphan) in the context of her late husband's estate. Two laws are concerned specifically with the status of the widow who has no living adult male relative to support her. The Middle Assyrian laws (ca. 1076 B. C., A 33) state, "If her husband and her father-in-law are both dead and she has no son, she becomes a widow, she may go where she wishes."[31] A woman whose husband has been captured and who has no father in law must wait two years before she may remarry. During these two years, the state is obligated to provide her support, at least to the value of her husband's estate, if she is in need (A 45). All the other laws deal with property disposition to the widow (Hammurabi 150, 171, 172, 176–177; Middle Assyrian A 25–26, 28, 33–35, 45–46; Neo-Babylonian, ca. 700 B. C., 12–13) or orphans (Lipit-Ishtar 24, 26–27, 31; Hammurabi 162, 173–174, 177; Middle Assyrian A 26, 28, 41; Neo-Babylonian 13, 15). These inheritance laws have several purposes: (a) to provide for the systematic transfer of property after the death of its owner and the succession of real property to the male children; (b) to support the widow for the rest of her life or until she remarries; (c) to maintain any minor children until they reach majority. Only three resources are subject to dispersal – the bride-price, the dowry, and the husband's/father's estate.[32]

No laws discuss what happens to poor widows and orphans – those who have no bride-price, dowry, or estate to support them. No mention is made of any payments for necessities from the king's treasury. Similarly, no laws exist on behalf of anyone else who is indigent. The needs of the poor are simply outside the purview of both law and government. As one scholar concludes, "The principle of the protection of the widows, orphans and the poor [that] appears in different prologues of the Mesopotamian laws […] is presented as a prescription without any legal sanction and consequently the chances of its application in actual life would seem to have been very limited."[33]

29 Havice: *Concern*, pp. 119–124.

30 Ibid., pp. 128–129.

31 Pritchard: *Texts*, p. 182.

32 Havice: *Concern*, pp. 130–131.

33 Epsztein: *Social Justice*, p. 16.

Ugarit

Ugarit was a city on the Mediterranean coast of modern Syria, which had its heyday from 1400 to 1200 B.C. Hundreds of clay tablets were discovered there upon which were written, among other things, fascinating polytheistic epics which cast light upon Canaanite mythology. Two texts refer to beneficence to the disadvantaged: In the Aqhat Legend, the king, Daniel, is depicted "sitting at the […] city-gate […] He judged the cause of the widow, made decisions regarding the orphan"; in the Kirta Epic, the king is condemned by his son who says that he does not deserve to reign because, "You judge not the cause of the widow, nor adjudicate the case of the oppressed, drive not out them that prey on the poor, feed not the orphan before you, the widow behind your back."[34] This latter reference is particularly reminiscent of the Egyptian kindness to the widow and orphan, and may indicate Egyptian influence.

Poverty in the Jewish Bible

It is important to realize that a variety of terms are used to indicate poverty in the Hebrew Bible.[35] The most common noun (or adjective) for a poor person in the Hebrew Bible is *ani*. Another noun of the same root *(ayin, nun, heh)* means "misery" which is how the word for "poor" originates. In other words, the connotations are of someone who is ill-treated, afflicted, humbled, or oppressed. Some other terms used are *evyon* (often translated as "needy"), *dal* ("weak"), and *rash* ("in want"). Additionally, certain phrases indicate impoverishment, such as "his hand cannot reach/attain" (Leviticus 5:7–13). The result is that poverty is referred to hundreds of times in the Jewish Bible. Since a comprehensive examination is beyond the scope of this paper, in this section we will look at the Biblical connections to the *condition* of poverty, irrespective of its particular terminology.

As indicated earlier, most occurrences of "widow" and "orphan" presume penury – the husband/father was the protector and bread-winner of the family and without him subsistence was precarious.

34 Havice: *Concern*, pp. 170–171. Similarly, a Hittite text states, "to the hungry give bread […] to the naked give clothing" (Moshe Weinfeld: *Social Justice in Ancient Israel and the Ancient Near East*. Jerusalem: Magnes 1995, p. 224).

35 See J. David Pleins: Poor, Poverty (Old Testament). In: *Anchor Bible Dictionary*, vol. 5, pp. 402–414.

Poverty in the Torah's Laws

The legal categories concerning poverty have parallels and differences with those of the stranger. The divergences are due to the fact that the poor, widow, and orphan are themselves full members of the people of Israel. With the exception of the few instances of inheritance laws, all the laws of the Torah concerning the poor have no parallel in ANE law.

General Admonitions: Do no harm; Do not subvert justice

"You shall not mistreat (the root *ayin*, *nun*, *heh*, see above) any widow or orphan. If you do mistreat him, I will heed his outcry as soon as he cries out to Me, and My anger shall blaze forth; I will kill you by the sword and your wives will be widows and your children orphans" (Exodus 22:21–23). The law is accentuated by a motive clause. Note the tit-for-tat correspondence between the lack of mercy by the Israelite to the victim, and God's punishment of the criminal. Deuteronomy 10:18 adds that it is God Himself who upholds the cause of the orphan and widow.

"You shall not subvert the rights of the needy in his dispute" (Exodus 23:6). The necessity of ensuring strict justice for each disputant, by not favoring one side over the other, is reinforced by verse 3, "You shall not show deference to a poor man in his dispute." The requirement for fairness in judgment is reiterated in Leviticus 19:15, "You shall not render an unfair judgment; Do not favor the poor or show deference to the rich. In righteousness you shall judge your kinsman" (compare Deuteronomy 1:16). Similarly, "Do not subvert the rights of the stranger or fatherless" (Deut. 24:17), and "Cursed be he who subverts the rights of the stranger, fatherless, and widow" (Deut. 27:19). The fact that the rights of the underprivileged are included in the twelve curses to be pronounced upon entry into the Promised Land is indicative of their abnormal importance.

Specific Laws of Social Justice

Prompt payment to the poor laborer: Deuteronomy 24:14–15 (including the stranger). The law is reiterated at the end of Leviticus 19:13, "The wages of a laborer shall not remain with you until morning." Day laborers were frequently poor and needed immediate payment to pay for necessities.

Free loans and returning of clothing as pledge by nightfall: "If you lend money to My people – to the poor among you – do not act towards them as a creditor; you must not exact interest from him. If you take your neighbor's garment from him in default of debt,[36] you must return it to him before the

36 See fn. 38.

sun sets, for it is his only clothing, the sole covering for his skin. In what (else) shall he sleep? Therefore, if he cries out to Me, I will pay heed, for I am compassionate" (Exodus 22:24–26). On the heels of verses 21–23, these verses give a specific example of how one is not to abuse the poor. In ancient Israel, people would only borrow money if they were in dire straits, as inability to pay back could entail debt-slavery.[37] The law concerning the pledge is replicated in Deuteronomy 24:12–13, with the additional exclusion of taking a widow's garment in default of debt (verse 17). Perhaps this exclusion is illustrative of the law's greater sensitivity to the widow's needs and dignity.[38] Deuteronomy 15:7–11 particularly encourages the giving of free loans,

> Should there be a needy person, one of your kinsman in any of your settlements in the land which the Lord your God is giving you, do not make your heart callous and shut your hand against your needy kinsman. Rather, you must open your hand to him and surely lend him sufficient for whatever he needs. Beware lest you harbor the base thought, "the seventh year, the year of remission, is approaching," so that you are mean to your needy kinsman and you give him nothing, and he will cry out to the Lord against you, and you will incur sin. Give to him readily and have no regrets when you do so, for in return the Lord your God will bless you in all your efforts and all your undertakings. For there will never cease to be needy ones in your land, which is why I command you, "Open your hand to the poor and needy kinsman in your land."

The reason that the Israelite may be reluctant to loan to the needy as the seventh year approaches is that the loan might end up as a gift, because the needy will not have enough time to either pay it back or work it off before the sabbatical year and the consequent remission of debts at that time. The text attempts to assure the lender that any loss will be more than made up for by God's bounty (similarly on the third year tithe, 14:29).[39]

37 Debt-slavery in the Bible and the ancient Near East was a common requirement when debtors were unable to pay their debts to their creditors. Such Israelites were enslaved to their Israelite creditors for a maximum of six years (Exodus 21:2; Deuteronomy 15:12). They were thus essentially different from permanent or chattel slaves. See further Muhammad A. Dandamayev: Slavery (OT), In: *Anchor Bible Dictionary*, vol. 6, pp. 62–65, here p. 63. For a more detailed survey see Gregory C. Chirichigno: *Debt-Slavery in Israel and the Ancient Near East*. Sheffield: JSOT 1993.

38 See Jeffrey Tigay: *Deuteronomy*. Philadelphia: Jewish Publication Society 1994, p. 228. That the Torah's law of not taking a poor laborer's garment in debt was known to the populace appears to be proven by the Mesad Hashavyahu ostracon, dated to the reign of Josiah (late 7th cent. B. C.), in which a reaper complains about the unjustified confiscation of his cloak (and see on Amos 2:8 below). See http://en.wikipedia.org/wiki/Mesad_Hashavyahu (accessed 01.07.2015).

39 Tigay: *Deuteronomy*, p. 147.

The law here against lending on interest is expanded upon in Leviticus 25:35–37: "If your kinsman becomes impoverished, and comes under your authority [...] do not exact from him advanced or accrued interest [interest deducted in advance or taken at the time of repayment], but you shall fear your God and let your kinsman live with you [that is, 'provide him with the means of subsistence since he is your kinsman and that is what God wants of you']. Do not lend him your money at advance interest, or give him your food at accrued interest." Deuteronomy 23:20–21 adds that no interest may be taken on anything else besides money and food (except to the foreigner which may be a reference to international trade), and includes a motive clause, "so that the Lord your God may bless you in all your undertakings in the land that you are entering to possess."

The law of Deuteronomy 15:7–11 actually contradicts verses 4–6:

> For there shall be no needy among you, for the Lord your God will bless you in the land that the Lord your God is giving you as a hereditary portion, if only you heed the Lord your God and take care to keep all these commandments that I command you this day. For the Lord your God will bless you as He has told you [...].

How can verse 7 state, "Should there be a needy person" when verse 4 says, "For there shall be no needy among you"? The answer is that the promise of verses 4–6 is conditional – if the people fully obey God's commandments, then He will so bless the land's produce that there will be plenty of food for everybody, that is, no one will be needy. Verses 7–11, on the other hand, indicate Deuteronomy's concession to reality. Disobedience will mean that the land's fertility will not be blessed by God, resulting in poverty. Nonetheless, those who take care of the poor will, in turn, be taken care of by the Lord.

Provision of food: Along with the stranger, the poor are included in the laws of the harvest gleanings and the third year tithe. Concerning the gleanings, Leviticus 19:10–11 and 23:22 mention the poor, while Deuteronomy 24:19–21 refers to the orphan and widow. The third year tithe in Deuteronomy 14:28–29 (and the farmer's affirmation in 26:12–13) also specifies the widow and orphan (as well as the Levite). The substitution of widow and orphan in Deuteronomy for the poor in Leviticus may be due to the perception in the former that the poor man can always be granted a loan and then can work off his debt, while the widow and orphan cannot. Thus, additional provision is made for the widow and orphan to obtain food.[40]

40 Jacob Milgrom: Leviticus 17–22. In: David N. Freedman (ed.): *Anchor Bible*. New York:

Additionally, the poor is provided for by the Exodus laws of the sabbatical year – "In the seventh year you shall let it [your land] rest and lie fallow. Let the needy among your people eat of it [...] you shall do the same with your vineyard and olive groves" (Exodus 23:11).[41]

As the Book of Ruth illustrates (Ruth 2:17), the gleanings at harvest time could, at least theoretically, provide food for a lengthy period of time. Thus, following the above laws may have enabled the poor to gather enough food to survive.

Redemption of the property of the poor: The poor have a prominent place in the laws of Leviticus 25, which deal with the sabbatical and jubilee (50th) years, as well as difficult circumstances in which the impoverished Israelite finds himself. Earlier, we referred to the free loan law in verses 35–37. Verses 25–28 apply to the destitute Israelite who has had to sell off his land, "If your kinsman becomes impoverished and sold part of his holding, his nearest redeemer [the closest relative who has the means to redeem the property] shall come and redeem what his kinsman has sold" (verse 25). The text then describes a situation in which the destitute Israelite gains enough funds to redeem the land himself. However, "If he lacks sufficient means to recover it [the land], what he sold shall remain with the purchaser until the jubilee; in the jubilee year it shall be released, and he shall return to his holding" (verse 28). The extraordinary institution of the jubilee year (like the sabbatical year, not known elsewhere in the ANE[42]) is designed to restore all property to the original family landowners (verses 10, 13–17), for the land is ultimately owned

Doubleday 2000, p. 1628. Milgrom, who understands Leviticus 17–27 to be the product of the Holiness source (H), also sees this source as reflecting the latter half of the 8th cent. B. C., a time when the family and clan structure was still strong enough in ancient Israel to provide care for the widow and orphan within those structures. However, a century later increasing urbanization and the dispossession of small farmers by the wealthy, with the resultant consolidation of small farms into large estates, resulted in the dissolution of the family and clan structure. That situation was reflected in Deuteronomy's promulgation of laws to provide food sources for the widow and orphan – in his view. Milgrom's detailed analysis of H appears on pp. 1319–1367.

41 It is to be noted that the sabbatical law in Leviticus 25:2–7 does *not* provide for all the poor, but may only be seen as providing for those for whom the householder is responsible, "*your male and female slaves, your hired laborers and your residents who sojourn with you*" (verse 6). It is questionable to whom "the residents" refer. Milgrom: Leviticus 23–27. In: David N. Freedman (ed.): *Anchor Bible*. New York: Doubleday 2001, p. 2160, explains that Leviticus has already provided for the general poor by the harvest laws of chapters 19 and 23.

42 Remission of debts and return of property occasionally occurred in proclamations of individual monarchs in the ANE, but there was nothing comparable to the recurring requirements of the Biblical sabbatical and jubilee years.

by God and cannot be sold in perpetuity (verse 23). The jubilee law was obviously intended to prevent a permanent economic imbalance in the social fabric due to the acquisition of large tracts of land by wealthy landowners.

The Israelite poor sold into slavery: Leviticus 25 also legislates two instances of the impoverished Israelite sold into slavery – when sold to another Israelite (verses 39–43, 46) and when sold to a prosperous resident alien (verses 47–55). The condition of the latter reflects the former. In both cases, the Israelite must be treated beneficially as a resident alien and must be released no later than the jubilee year, whereupon he returns to his family and ancestral holding. Similar laws, but without identifying the Israelite slave as impoverished, appear in Exodus 21:1–11 and Deuteronomy 15:12–18, where the maximum term of servitude is six years. In the Hammurabi Laws #117, the term for debt-slavery is listed as three years, although if the debtor provides a slave to work out the debt, the term can be longer (#118).

Both laws contain motive clauses, "For they are My slaves whom I freed from the land of Egypt; they may not be sold as slaves are sold [that is, forever]. You shall not rule over them ruthlessly; you shall fear your God" (verses 42–43; see also verses 46, 55). These motive clauses reminding the Israelites that God freed them from slavery not only serve to negate the possibility of holding an Israelite slave permanently, but also forbid mistreating him because the word "ruthlessly" is the very term used in Exodus 1:13–14 to describe the harsh labor imposed upon the Israelites by the Egyptians.

The law on the sale of an Israelite to a resident alien further emphasizes that, since the Israelites belong to God, it is not becoming that an Israelite be a slave to a non-Israelite. Therefore, everything should be done to redeem him quickly (verses 48–49).

The widow and orphan must be included in holiday rejoicing: Along with the stranger and the slave, during the holidays of the Feast of Weeks and Tabernacles (Deuteronomy 16:11, 14). The motivational statement of verse 12 is of particular importance, "You shall remember that you were a slave in Egypt – take care to observe these laws." The fact that "you" in verse 12 is in the singular is a cogent pointer to each Israelite to bear in mind that he was a slave, that is, that each Israelite was a member of the weakest, poorest, most downtrodden segment of society.[43] As such, the Israelite must be always conscious that, just as God cared about him, he must care about the deprived members of society.

43 Similarly, the declaration in Deut. 26:6–7.

Moral and Ritual Law, Positive and Negative Commandments

Since the poor, widow, and orphan are all Israelites, they are obligated to the same laws as the rest of the people. However, sacrificial law takes their poverty into cognizance and significantly readjusts the purification offering (for sin) to substitute two turtledoves or pigeons for a sheep or goat, and if that is still too costly, the individual may bring a cereal offering (equivalent to the value of a day's bread, Leviticus 5:7–13). Similar laws concern the indigent woman who gives childbirth (12:6–8), the poor person who is leprous and brings a reparation offering (14:21–32), and the penurious vower (27:8). These cultic allowances for poverty, though, are not unique in the ancient world.[44]

Inheritance Laws

In resemblance to the Mesopotamian laws mentioned above, inheritance laws protected the rights of widows and orphans: inheritance of the first-born son (Deuteronomy 21:15–17); levirate marriage (where the brother of the deceased husband, who leaves no son, marries the widow, Deuteronomy 25:5–10). Further, a widow (or divorcee) is a free agent to impose a vow upon herself (without being checked by a father or husband, Numbers 30:10).

The levirate marriage law has affinities to: the legal case of the daughters of Zelophehad, whose father died leaving neither son nor brother (Numbers 27:1–11, 36:1–12; Joshua 17:3–6); the story in Genesis 38, in which Judah refused to give his daughter-in-law Tamar to his youngest son after the older two died; Ezekiel's prophecy that priests may marry the widows of other priests (Ezekiel 44:22); the marriage of the widow Ruth to Boaz, a kinsman of her husband (Ruth 3:1–4:17).

In sum, the Torah's laws differ from those of the ANE by not only demanding justice and protection for the poor, but also requiring that the poor be provided with free loans (even if they will not be repaid), several means of obtaining food, options for redemption from debt slavery, and restoration of property in the jubilee year. Particularly, the laws of free loans and the right of the poor to glean after the harvesters will eventually evolve into the

44 Milgrom: Leviticus 1–16. In: David Noel Freedman (ed.): *Anchor Bible*. New York: Doubleday 1998, pp. 304–307. Milgrom notes the existence of a 3rd cent. B.C. Punic text that also records a concession to the indigent (p. 304), and a similar statement in Mesopotamia, "the widow makes her offering to you (plural) with cheap flour, the rich man with a lamb" (p. 862). It should also be noted that the half-shekel offering in Exodus 30:11–16 is the same for rich and poor (verse 15).

requirement in later Jewish law to give the poor money. Given the Torah's ethical stance on the poor, it is no coincidence that the term for this giving will be the Hebrew *tzedakah* – the Biblical word for "righteousness." This evolution will already be seen in certain Biblical texts outside the Torah (below).

Poverty in the Torah's Laws Reflected in the Rest of the Jewish Bible

Terms for poverty, including references to widows and orphans, appear some 250 times in the Hebrew Bible outside of the Torah's laws, including about 75 times in prophecy – far more material than this work can cover. Unquestionably, then, poverty is a major subject in the Jewish Bible, with many ramifications, such as: allegories about poor people used as object lessons in 2 Samuel (the poor man's ewe lamb in relation to Uriah – 12:1–7; the widow's son in relation to Absalom – 14:4–21); the prophets Elijah and Elisha each help feed a poor widow and her progeny;[45] the psalmist claims poverty and affliction and pleads to God for forgiveness and/or deliverance;[46] the wicked oppress the poor,[47] but God saves them;[48] even the entire people are referred to as poor.[49]

Further, many Biblical passages reiterate the Mesopotamian theme of the protection of the poor, weak, widow, and orphan from the strong and wealthy,[50] as well as the additional Egyptian emphasis on feeding the hungry and clothing the naked.[51] Again, in parallel to the appearance of this theme in ANE hymns/petitions and wisdom literature, it is no coincidence that many Biblical occurrences are found in the hymns/petitions of Psalms, and the wisdom books of Proverbs and Job.

This brief section, then, will focus primarily on examples of the influence of the Torah's legislation on later texts.

The use of specific language in the prophets copies the general admonitions in the Torah:

The prohibitions not to "*subvert the right*" of the needy (Exodus 23:6) and the orphan (and stranger – Deuteronomy 24:17, along with the curse of

45 1 Kings 17:8–24; 2 Kings 4:1–7.

46 Psalms 25:16–18, 40:18, 86:1–5.

47 Isaiah 3:15, 32:6–7; Psalms 10:2, 9, 37:14; Job 24:14.

48 Zephaniah 3:12; Psalm 12:6, 14:6, 35:10; Proverbs 22:22–23.

49 Isaiah 26:1–6 – in which the people are also identified as righteous, 49:13; Psalm 18:28, 72:2.

50 Isaiah 1:17; Jeremiah 20:13, 22:16; Psalm 72:1–2, 4, 12; Prov. 29:7, 31:9; Job 29:16, 31:21; etc.

51 Isaiah 58:6–7; Psalm 132:15; Prov. 22:9; Job 31:19; etc.

one who subverts the right of the widow, orphan, and stranger in 27:19), reverberates in Amos (usually dated to 775–750 B.C.) 5:11–12, "*because you levy a straw tax on the poor and exact a grain tax from him* [...] *and you subvert (the right) of the needy in the gate*" (courts of justice sat at the gate of the city). Similarly, Isaiah (approx. 725–700 B.C.) 10:2 discusses the negative effect of the decrees of wicked authorities, "*to subvert the case of the weak and to rob the rights of the poor of My people, so that widows may be their booty, and they will despoil orphans.*" Likewise, Malachi (early 5th century B.C.) 3:5 depicts God's anger against those who subvert the rights of the widow and orphan.[52]

The particular language used in Deuteronomy 24:14 of not to "abuse"[53] the poor and needy hired laborer (whether Israelite or stranger) is echoed by the prophets in Jeremiah (approx. 620–580 B.C.) 7:6, "(If) you do not abuse the stranger, orphan, and widow" and Zechariah (525–500 B.C.) 7:10, "Do not abuse the widow, orphan, stranger, and poor". In Amos 4:1, greedy wealthy wives "abuse the weak and crush the needy."[54]

Apparently, the close proximity of the prohibition not to "afflict" the stranger in Exodus 22:20 with that of not to "mistreat" the widow and orphan in verses 21–22 (the words in Hebrew are also close in sound) influenced later prophetic texts: "Do not afflict the stranger, orphan, and widow" (Jeremiah 22:3); "They abused the stranger [...] they afflicted the orphan and widow," "They afflicted the poor and needy and they abused the stranger" (Ezekiel (600–570 B.C.) 22:7, 29).

Specific Torah legislation concerning the poor is reflected in a passage in Amos. In a prophecy against the northern kingdom of Israel, the prophet predicts destruction due to moral crimes, "because they have sold [...] the needy for a pair of sandals. [Those] who [even] desire the dust on the head of the poor, and thrust the humble off the road[55] [...] Upon garments seized in

52 A similar idea appears in the 7th century B.C. Hymn to Shamash (lines 41–47) in which the god intercedes on behalf of the weak to ensure justice – Pritchard: *Texts*, p. 388. The relatively late date of this text shows that it could not have influenced Amos or Isaiah. Geo-politically, it could not have influenced Malachi either since the Hymn was found in Assyria and Malachi lived in Persian-controlled Judah.

53 The Hebrew word *ashok*.

54 Further, see Psalms 72:4, 146:7; Proverbs 14:31, 22:16, 28:3.

55 Compare Job 24:4, "*They push the needy off the road.*"

for default of debt[56], they stretch themselves out beside every altar" – (Amos, 2:6–8; cf. 8:6). Amos here draws upon Exodus 22:25, "If you take your neighbor's clothing in default of debt, you must return it to him by sunset" (similarly, Deuteronomy 24:17, "Do not take a widow's garment in default of debt"). The idea of stretching themselves out besides altars on garments taken from the poor adds insult to injury (whether or not these altars are those of God). Nowhere else in the ANE is there a reference to the taking of garments in default of debt.

Two Historical Accounts

Jeremiah 34:8–22 and Nehemiah 5:1–13 provide us with two historical accounts of social upheaval that reflect the Torah's laws concerning the poor, particularly concerning the sabbatical and jubilee years.[57]

Jeremiah 34:8–22: In this famous passage, at the time when the Babylonian siege of Jerusalem (588–587 B. C.) had been temporarily lifted, King Zedekiah of Judah makes a covenant with the people of Jerusalem "*to proclaim liberty to them*" (that is, a complete release of all their Hebrew slaves) (verses 8–9). The phrase "to proclaim liberty" hearkens back to Leviticus 25:10[58] concerning the jubilee year – "*you shall proclaim liberty throughout the land to all its inhabitants.*"[59] Perhaps, Zedekiah hoped that, by effecting the release of all the Hebrew slaves, God would bless the people and save the city from the Babylonians – as it says in Deuteronomy 15:6, if the people heed God's commands "*the Lord your God will bless you as He has promised you* [...] *you will rule over many nations and they shall not rule over you.*"

Initially, the Jerusalemites obey the covenant and release their slaves. However, in a short while, they recapture those who were set free and force them back into slavery (verses 10–11). This heinous behavior prompts Jeremiah to prophesy (verses 12–14), "*Thus says the Lord, the God of Israel: I made a covenant with your fathers when I brought them out of the land of Egypt, the house of bondage, saying, 'In the seventh year each of you must let go any fellow Hebrew who may be sold to you; when he has served you six years, you must set him free'*". In these verses, Jeremiah paraphrases Deuteronomy 15, verses 1, 12–15, and 18 concerning the

56 See Shalom Paul: *Amos*, *Hermeneia*. Minneapolis: Fortress 1991, p. 83.

57 See Milgrom's cogent arguments, id.: Leviticus 23–27, pp. 2257–2270.

58 The only other places, outside of this verse and Jeremiah 34, in which the Hebrew word for liberty, *dror*, appears are the later texts of Isaiah 61:1 and Ezekiel 46:17.

59 As is well known, these words (with a slightly different translation) are inscribed on the Liberty Bell.

requirement in the sabbatical year laws to let debt-slaves go free (and see also Leviticus 25:39–43, 46 above). Now, Jeremiah (verses 15–17) draws on the laws of the jubilee year in Leviticus 25 in pronouncing God's judgment:

> Recently, you [...] did that which was right in My eyes [...] to proclaim liberty each man to his fellow [...] but now you have profaned My name; each man has brought back his male and female slaves whom you set free, and you have forced them back to be your male and female slaves [again]. Therefore, thus says the Lord: you would not obey Me to proclaim liberty each person to his kinsman and countryman, then I proclaim liberty, declares the Lord, to the sword, and the pestilence, and the famine, and I will make you a horror to all the kingdoms of the earth.

Jeremiah then culminates the prophecy with the promise of the destruction of Jerusalem and the rest of Judah by the Babylonians, and the death of all those who violated the covenant (verses 18–22).

Nehemiah 5:1–13: In contrast to the failed attempt at slave-release in Jeremiah 34, some 150 years later, an extraordinary event without parallel in the ancient world takes place in Nehemiah 5 (perhaps 438–437 B.C.). Persia now rules the Middle East. Cyrus the Great had allowed the return of the Jews to the Land of Israel in 539–538 B.C., after he had conquered Babylon. By 515 B.C., the Temple in Jerusalem had been rebuilt, although on a much more humble scale than had existed under the Davidic monarchy. By the middle of the 5th century B.C., the Jewish population of Judah was in dire economic straits, and the walls of Jerusalem – destroyed by Babylon – were still in ruins. Nehemiah, a Jew, is cupbearer (possibly indicative of high office, in similarity to the cupbearer of Pharaoh in Genesis 40) to the Persian king, Artaxerxes I (465–424 B.C.). Devastated by the sad news of the state of Judah and Jerusalem, Nehemiah requests to go on a mission to Judah to rebuild Jerusalem. Not only does the king grant him official permission, but he makes Nehemiah governor of Judah. Nehemiah journeys to Jerusalem and begins rebuilding the walls.

It is at this time that Nehemiah 5 opens with the outcry of the impoverished Judeans, heard by Nehemiah (verses 1–5). The common people lack food, have pawned their property to their wealthier coreligionists, and, due to having had to pay the royal tax, their children are being taken into debt-slavery. Thus, the common folk are not only impoverished, but they have no way to redeem their debts. At this moment of crisis, Nehemiah calls a plenary assembly to win popular support and, thereby, to force the creditors to take immediate action on behalf of their poor brethren.[60] He calls upon them to stop their unethical behavior, to forego all that is still owed, and to return all property taken in default of the debts. Amazingly, they do so (verses 6–13)! One, highly impressed, contemporary scholar says that, in the ancient world, this incident is

> the most complete paradigm of what is meant by social justice as distinct from righteousness or the call to upright living […] social justice is clearly a form of justice involving different classes of society and not between individuals. In this case, […] the lower classes apparently had a recognized right of complaint […] to the ruler […] the upper classes voluntarily, and without any sanction, yielded justice and restored the possessions of the poor. The appeal of the poor had been made on the basis of the equality of those different classes (Nehemiah 5:5).
>
> This single incident differs from all others in the ancient and medieval worlds. While our knowledge about the reforms of […] [others] is extensive, there is not the slightest indication that the lower classes enjoyed a recognized right to demand social justice, and certainly, in almost all cases, the upper classes refused to concede voluntarily any rights to the oppressed.[61]

To understand the Torah's influence, it is worthwhile pointing out the connections between Nehemiah 5 and the laws of Leviticus 25:[62]

The motivational statement in Nehemiah 5:9, "*What you are doing is not right. You ought to act in a God-fearing way.*"

Leviticus 25:43, "*You shall not rule over him ruthlessly, but you shall fear your God.*"[63]

Restitution of property, as required in the jubilee year, with the verb "to return" – Neh. 5:11–12; Lev. 25:25–28, 41.

Prohibition of treating fellow Israelites like slaves – Neh. 5:8; Lev. 25:39, 46.

Prohibition against taking interest – Neh. 5:11; Lev. 25:36.

60 Joseph Blenkinsopp: *Ezra – Nehemiah, Old Testament Library.* Philadelphia: Westminster 1988, p. 259.

61 Howard L. Adelson: The Origins of a Concept of Social Justice. In: K. D. Irani / Morris Silver (eds): *Social Justice in the Ancient World.* Westport, CT: Westview 1995, pp. 25–38, here pp. 25–26.

62 Blenkinsopp: *Ezra,* p. 259.

63 Also, Lev. 25:17, 36.

Even if one were to challenge the historical accuracy of both Jeremiah 34 and Nehemiah 5, it is indisputable that the authors of both accounts are influenced by the Torah's legislation on behalf of the poor.

Conclusions on the Concern for the Poor in the Jewish Bible

The desire to protect the poor and weak from exploitation by the strong and wealthy is pervasive in ANE literature, and the particular ethic of sustaining the impoverished is a characteristic of Egyptian literature. Additionally, these virtues were seen to be a concern of the gods and were initially directed at the monarchs and their officials. In Egyptian society, eventually, such behavior was seen as meritorious by all who had the means. Failure to care for the needy would make the individual liable to be punished by the gods.

The Jewish Bible, while echoing similar concerns as the surrounding cultures, moves this state of affairs to a more advanced ethical level. *For the first time, the obligation of each member of the society to care for and sustain the poor is enshrined in law.*[64] More than that, *new laws are created on behalf of the poor* which are unattested by any kind of societal behavior elsewhere: free loans, tithes, harvest gleanings,[65] the return of property at the jubilee, regular cancellation of debts, regular release from slavery, the Sabbath rest (incumbent upon all), and partaking in festival celebrations.

Of particular significance are the laws providing food for the poor, including the needy resident alien. The ancient world was constantly under the threat of drought, food shortages, and famine, where subsistence living was often, if not generally, the norm.[66] In such a world, the Jewish Bible is the first text

64 Havice's claim, that the Torah's law on behalf of the needy is often an authoritarian appeal that assumes that the hearer is an ethically incompetent actor (Havice: *Concern*, pp. 229–247), is indefensible. No society can exist without legal requirements. The enshrinement of ethical values within a society's law code, requiring specific actions and attitudes, is far greater evidence of the importance of those values than if they were simply left as suggestions. Consider the difference in safe driving between signs on the freeways which might read "For your own safety and that of others, the State recommends that you do not exceed 65 miles per hour" and the knowledge that one could get a severe fine for speeding. Havice, apparently, has to bend over backward to prove that Israel's unique laws on behalf of the disadvantaged do not represent an ethical advancement over the rest of the ANE.

65 Even though an individual widow may have received permission to glean in a specific field (see the Instructions of Amenemope cited above), there is no evidence that this was a societal custom.

66 See Peter Garnsey: *Food and Society in Classical Antiquity*. Cambridge: Cambridge UP 1999; id.: *Famine and Food Supply in the Graeco-Roman World: Responses to Risk and Crisis*. Cambridge: Cambridge UP 1988; id.: *Cities, Peasants, and Food in Classical Antiquity: Essays in Social and Economic*

to legislate food supplies for the poor. The advantage of these laws for the needy cannot be overestimated. While other societies only attempted to deal with food shortages and famine when crises occurred, the Torah's regulations afford continual relief to the destitute.

Even these ethical progressions do not tell the whole story. One must always remember the Biblical claim that its laws are not only given by God, but are themselves the stipulations of the Sinai treaty. Thus, not only will the people as individuals be rewarded or punished conditional upon their obedience or disobedience, but the future of the entire society is decided thereby. Therefore, as seen in the verses cited above, Deuteronomy promises God's blessings on the entire society for generosity to the poor. At the same time, the verses of the prophets cited above – Amos, Isaiah, Jeremiah, Ezekiel, Malachi – all appear within prophecies that decree destruction due to the abuse of the rights of the needy. *The idea that the destiny of a society is determined by how its members behave to the needy is a Biblical invention* – and prefigures the modern, ethical conceptions of government, ranging from democracy to socialism, to create societies in which the needs of the impoverished will be met.[67]

History. Cambridge: Cambridge UP 1998, particularly pp. 183–292. I thank Dr. Yehiel Leiter for these references. Democratic Athens created a continuous system of food distribution only in the 4th Cent. B. C. (Gamsey: *Famine and Food Supply*, pp. 30, 144). Otherwise, societies had to rely on the largess of the upper classes during times of famine (Gamsey: *Food and Society*, p. 33; id.: *Cities, Peasants, and Food*, p. 274).

67 I wish to thank the seminar members at the Institute for Advanced Studies (housed then at Shalem College, but later at the Herzl Institute), before whom I presented this section on the poor (June 11, 2013), for pointing this out to me. It should be noted that the concept of destruction due to immorality is not completely unknown in Mesopotamian literature. An ancient Babylonian wisdom text, *Advice to a Prince*, states "If a king does not heed justice [...] his land will be devastated [...] If citizens of Nippur are brought before him for judgment and he accepts bribe and treats them with injustice, Enlil [...] will bring a foreign army against him." In other words, the king will be punished and may even lose his throne for his own immoral acts. Note that this text does not refer to national destruction and/or exile. Nor is it a legal text, although the king's responsibility for moral order is well known. Similarly, the Esarhaddon (king of Assyria, 680–669 B. C.) inscriptions attempt to justify the destruction of Babylon (by Esarhaddon's father, Sennacherib, in 689 B. C.): the Babylonians "plotted evil [...] were oppressing the weak/poor [...] they were robbing each other's property; the son was cursing his father in the street [...] then the god (Enlil/Marduk) became angry, he planned to overwhelm the land and to destroy its people." Note that the king of Assyria, after the fact, imputes widespread moral decay to the Babylonian enemy to explain the god's decision to destroy Babylon (thus, absolving his father). Although this late sentiment, at face value, accords with earlier Biblical thought, this inscription is hardly comparable to the Torah's prospective legislation and admonitions or to the prophets' prophecies of doom. See Moshe Weinfeld: Ancient Near Eastern Patterns in Prophetic Literature. In: *Vetus Testamentum* 27 (1977), pp. 178–195, here pp. 194–195.

"We Were Extremely Poor but We Were Pious"

Exploring the Relationships between Religious Adherence and Economic Status in the Muslim World

Logan Cochrane / Waleed Chellan

Introduction

Lives that are more comfortable and secure have less need for religion, Pippa Norris and Ronald Inglehart argue.[1] There is no need for religion, Phil Zuckerman believes, particularly when physical, economic and social security as well as political stability develop.[2] Are people religious due to insecurities, anxieties and stress, as Tomas James Rees and Gregory Paul suggest,[3] an opiate masking the true realities of life? This paper provides insight into these questions by analyzing theological, quantitative and qualitative components influencing the relationships between economic status and religious adherence.

Surveys conducted in 114 countries around the world find that the majority of all people, eighty-four percent, say that religion is an important part of their daily lives.[4] That survey also found that the most religious countries were those that were relatively poor.[5] There are only few countries with a majority of the population that are secular and are relatively poor, China and Vietnam are two examples. Alternatively, the United States is an example of a country with a high GDP per capita wherein the majority feels that religion is important in their daily lives, which is also the case in Italy and Ireland.[6] These irregularities have resulted in some researchers revisiting the

1 Pippa Norris / Ronald Inglehart: *Sacred and Secular: Religion and Politics Worldwide*. Cambridge: Cambridge UP 2004.

2 Phil Zuckerman: *Society Without God: What the Least Religious Nations Can Tell Us about Contentment*. New York: New York UP 2010.

3 Tomas James Rees: Is Personal Insecurity a Cause of Cross-National Differences in the Intensity of Religious Belief? In: *Journal of Religion and Society* 11 (2009), pp. 1–24, here p. 12; Gregory Paul: The Chronic Dependence of Popular Religiosity upon Dysfunctional Psychosociological Conditions. In: *Evolutionary Psychology* 7,3 (2009), pp. 398–441, here p. 421.

4 Steven Crabtree: Religiosity Highest in World's Poorest Nations. http://www.gallup.com/poll/142727/religiosity-highest-world-poorest-nations.aspx (accessed 31.12.2014).

5 "Relatively poor" was marked as having an average per capita GDP below US $5,000.

6 Norris / Inglehart: *Sacred and Secular*.

underlying assumptions that predicted the inevitable decline of religion and religious life.

Although the explanations have changed, from modernization and secularization theories to coping mechanisms, the story remains largely the same: higher religious adherence is connected to lower economic status. In 2004 Norris and Inglehart suggested that people in countries with lower economic statuses face greater levels of vulnerability and therefore adhere to religion at higher levels as a means of attaining and retaining hope. While this work reframed the question, it is in many ways grounded in similar assumptions put forward by Karl Marx, Max Weber and Émile Durkheim; as life improves, religion will be less and less important. Gallup suggests that its survey findings support this theory; it presents data on the role of religion as enhancing enjoyment and reducing negative emotions, which, they argue, demonstrates the positive role that religion plays for those living more economically challenging lives.[7] Thus, religion has utility for those living in poverty, and remains therefore important for them.

The challenge with correlations is that they are correlations, not causations; many different correlations regarding religious adherence have been made. For example, religious adherence has been correlated with life satisfaction and happiness, which can be correlated with social connectivity and social capital.[8] Just as the ways in which religious adherence is reexamined, so too are concepts of well-being; some research suggests that economic status influences emotional well-being and life evaluation in different ways.[9] The trend of recent research is to engage in a more nuanced analysis of the correlations between economic status and religious adherence, and it is to this body

7 Steve Crabtree / Brett Pelham: Religion Provides Emotional Boost to World's Poor. http://www.gallup.com/poll/116449/Religion-Provides-Emotional-Boost-World-Poor.aspx (accessed 31.12.2014).

8 Numerous and diverse studies explore these relationships, some recent publications include Chaeyoon Lima / Robert D. Putnam: Religion, Social Networks, and Life Satisfaction. In: *American Sociological Review* 75,5 (2010), pp. 914–933; Christofer Edling / Jens Rydgren / Love Bohman: Faith or Social Foci? Happiness, Religion, and Social Networks in Sweden. In: *European Sociological Review* 30,5 (2014), pp. 615–626; Ryan S. Ritter / Jesse Lee Preston / Ivan Hernandez: Happy Tweets: Christians are Happier, More Socially Connected, and Less Analytical than Atheists on Twitter. In: *Social Psychology and Personality Science* 5,2 (2014), pp. 243–249; Shigehiro Oishi / Ed Diener: Residents of Poor Nations Have a Greater Sense of Meaning in Life than Residents of Wealthy Nations. In: *Psychological Science* 25,2 (2014), pp. 422–430.

9 Daniel Kahneman / Angus Deaton: High Income Improves Evaluation of Life but not Emotional Well-being. In: *Proceedings of the National Academy of Science of the United States of America* 107,38 (2010), pp. 16489–16493, here p. 16490.

of literature that this study aims to contribute. The first section in this paper explores the concept of poverty from a theological perspective. The second section uses quantitative national data, drawn from a thirty-nine country dataset, to assess correlations between gross domestic product (GDP) per capita, promotion of religion as means to organize society and levels of individual religious practice. The third section provides qualitative life-history data to explore the lived experiences of religion, religious adherence and wealth, or lack thereof.

Poverty as an Islamic Concept[10]

In its most common use, living in poverty is defined as a state wherein one has an insufficiency of capital and/or material possessions.[11] While the elimination and reduction of poverty are both a part of the rights of individuals and a responsibility of society within Islamic Law (sharīʿah),[12] it is theologically expected that some will have more than others.[13] The notion of protecting individual financial wellbeing is enshrined in the five core higher objectives (maqāṣid) of sharīʿah namely: protection of faith, person, progeny, property and intellect.[14] One of the societal reasons why individual poverty ought to be reduced is because such a state may result, encourage or necessitate in irreligious or criminal activity. However, the value of a person is not a reflection of his or her wealth, rather, the Qur'an states that individuals are distinguished from one another only on the basis of their piety.[15] Many

10 Islam is an Abrahamic faith that confirms the Prophets of the past and emphasizes monotheism. During much of the last fourteen hundred years, Islam has been the predominant faith from Morocco to Pakistan as well as in large parts of Central Asia and Southeast Asia. As minorities, Muslims live throughout the rest of the world. Approximately a quarter of the global population adheres to Islam; 1.6 billion people. Islamic practice is defined by five key pillars: the profession of faith (shahādah), ritual prayer (ṣalāh), alms giving (zakāh), fasting the month of Ramadan (ṣawm), and pilgrimage (ḥajj). For an assumption on Muslim future see Pew Forum: *The Future of the Global Muslim Population.* Washington: Pew Research Center's Forum on Religion & Public Life 2011.

11 Muḥammad Ibn Jarīr al-Ṭabarī: *Jāmiʿu al-Bayān fī Taʾwīl al-Qurʾān* [*An Extensive Presentation on the Exegesis of the Quran*]. Beirut: Muʾassasah al-Risālah liʾl-Ṭabāʿāt waʾl-Nashr waʾl-Tawzīʿ 2000.

12 Ismail Sirageldin: Elimination of Poverty: Challenges and Islamic Strategies. In: *Islamic Economic Studies* 8,1 (2000), pp. 1–16, here p. 2.

13 Qur'an 16:71: "and God has favored some of you over others in provision".

14 ʾIbrāhīm Ibn Mūsā al-Shāṭibī: *al-Muwāfaqāt fī Uṣūl al-Sharīʿah* [*The Reconciliation of the Fundamentals of Islamic Law*]. Al-Khubar: Dār Ibn ʿAffān 1997.

15 Qur'an 49:13: "Indeed the most noble of you in the sight of God is the most righteous of you."

faith traditions, including Islam, distinguish between different forms of poverty, wherein some states of poverty are desirable and others are detested. The challenge of negotiating these forms of poverty is explored by Osman Guner, who illustrates a number of the theological manifestations of poverty.[16] The first, insufficient economic and material possessions, and the second, spiritual poverty, are both definitions that are derived from the Qur'an. Economic and material poverty have different manifestations, as outlined in the Qur'an. Of the most prominent, there are differentiations made between the poor (fuqarā') and the destitute (masākīn), and that of chronic and temporary poverty, examples of the latter include the wayfarer (ibn al-sabīl) and overburdened (ghārimīn).[17] The next distinction Guner derives is from the Prophetic narrations, which differentiates asceticism (zuhd) from material poverty. While the two may outwardly appear similar, the former is an intentionally impoverished life lived as a means to draw near to God.

The deconstruction of poverty from a theological perspective is not the objective here, indeed volumes have been written on the subject.[18] Rather, the outlining of these different conceptualizations of poverty within Islamic theology are presented in order to contextualize the quantitative and qualitative data in the sections that follow, particularly with regard to the lack of this form of analysis within quantitative data sets. There is not only a lack of distinguishing between asceticism and economic and material poverty, but also the different manifestations of economic and material poverty itself (relative, chronic and temporary forms of poverty).

In the Prophetic narrations material and economic poverty are warned against. One Prophetic supplication includes: "I seek refuge with You from poverty"[19], and believers are encouraged to "seek refuge with God from poverty".[20] The body of narrations also warns against wealth, which is not

16 Osman Guner: Poverty in Traditional Islamic Thought: Is It Virtue or Captivity? In: *Studies in Islam and the Middle East* 2,1 (2005), pp 1–12, here pp. 2–6.

17 Karima Korayem / Neamat Mashhour: Poverty in Secular and Islamic Economics: Conceptualization and Poverty Alleviation, with Reference to Egypt. In: *Topics in Middle Eastern and African Economies* 16,1 (2014), pp. 1–16, here pp. 3–6.

18 Yūsuf Al-Qaraḍāwī: *Mushkilah al-Faqr wa Kayfa 'Ālijuhā al-'Islām* [*The Problem of Poverty and How to Address it*]. Beirut: Mu'assasah al-Risālah li'l-Ṭabā'āt wa'l-Nashr wa'l-Tawzī' 1985; 'Abd al-Raḥmān Bin Sa'd Bin 'Abd al-Raḥmān Āli Sa'ūd: *Mushkilah al-Faqr wa Subul 'Ilājuhā fī Ḍaw'i al-'Islām* [*The Problem of Poverty and the Ways of its Treatment in Light of Islam*]. Riyadh: Dār al-Nashr bi'l-Markaz al-'Arabī li'l-Dirāsah al-'Amniyya wa'l-Tadrīb 1990.

19 Abū 'Abd al-Raḥmān al-Nasā'ī. Sunan al-Nasā'ī: *Kitāb al-'isti'ādhah ,bāb al-'isti'ādhah min al-dhillah*. Aleppo: Maktab al-Maṭbū'āt al-'Islāmiyyah 1986.

20 Aḥmad Ibn Ḥanbal: *Musnad al-'Imām Aḥmad Ibn Ḥanbal, Musnad Abū Hurayrah, ḥadīth 10973*. Beirut: Mu'assasah al-Risālah li'l-Ṭabā'āt wa'l-Nashr wa'l-Tawzī' 2001.

theologically problematic in and of itself, rather it is what one does with that wealth that makes it desirable or detested. Particularly interesting in these narrations is the link between material wealth and spiritual poverty, which echoes the Gallup findings regarding religious adherence and economic status globally. One Prophetic narration states: "By God I do not fear for you poverty, but I fear that you will lead a life of luxury as the past nations did, whereupon you will compete for it as they competed for it, and it will destroy you as it has destroyed them."[21] The respected medieval exegete Ibn Ḥajar (d. 1449) explained that the meaning of destruction in this narration relates to a spiritual one, stating: "we assume that it shows that the harm of poverty is unlike the harm of affluence, since in most instances the harm of poverty is limited to the worldly life while the harm of affluence mostly manifests in the afterlife."[22] Ibn Ḥajar adds, quoting Ibn Baṭṭāl (d. 1054), that often "affluence is a symbol of having fallen into the trap (of the worldly life) which leads to the destruction of the soul."[23] While other exegetes might debate these explanations, there are supporting Prophetic narrations that suggest this destruction includes a spiritual component. For example, on one occasion some of the companions of Prophet Muhammad were speaking about their fear of poverty, to which he responded: "Is it poverty that you fear? By the One in Whose Hand is my soul, this world will come to you in plenty, and nothing will cause the heart of anyone of you to deviate except that."[24] While these narrations do not specify the exact nature of the relationship between economic status and religious adherence, these theological sources suggest that the existence of such a relationship would not be contrary to them, and that such a finding might even be expected.

21 Muḥammad Ibn 'Ismā'īl al-Bukhārī: *Ṣaḥīḥ al-Bukhārī, kitāb al-maghāẓī, bāb shuhūd al-malā'ikah badrā, ḥadīth 4015*. Beirut: Dār Ṭūq al-Najjāt 2001; Muslim Ibn al-Ḥajjāj: *Ṣaḥīḥ Muslim, kitāb al-ẓuhd wa'l-raqā'iq, ḥadīth 2961*. Beirut: Dār 'Iḥyā' al-Turāth al-'Arabī 1991; Abū 'Īsā al-Tirmidhī: *Sunan al-Tirmidhī, abwāb ṣiffah al-qiyāmah wa'l-raqā'iq wa'l-war', ḥadīth 2462*. Cairo: Sharikah Maktabah wa Maṭba'ah Muṣṭafā al-Bābī al-Ḥalbī 1975.

22 Ibn Ḥajar al-'Asqalānī: *Fatḥ al-Bārī [Provisions of the Creator], kitāb al-riqāq, bāb mā yuḥdharu min ẓaharah al-dunyā' wa'l-tanāfus fīhā, ḥadith 6425*. Cairo: Dār al-Bayān al-'Arabī (nd).

23 Ibid.

24 Ibn Mājah al-Qazwīnī: *Sunan Ibn Mājah, abwāb al-sunnah, bāb 'ittibā' sunnah rasūl Allāh, ḥadīth 5*. Damascus: Dār al-Risālah al-'Ālamiyyah 2009.

Poverty and Islam Globally

The use of quantitative macro-level data to understand the relationship between economic status and religious adherence is challenged by a lack of data and of data selection processes. The former relates to an insufficient amount of data on degrees of religious adherence, and in the event of data being available, there are problems related to inconsistencies of collection methodologies as well as different forms of religious adherence being investigated. Due to these limitations, one must determine which data ought to be used for analysis; this poses a potential problem of biased selection. To take a simplistic example, one might justify the claim that poorer people are more religious using national data from Senegal, where more than 94 percent of the population practice Islam,[25] gross domestic product per capita is $2,242 (155th of 185 nations),[26] a third of the population lives in extreme poverty,[27] and almost two thirds live on less than two dollars a day.[28] The opposite claim might be justified using data from Qatar, where a large majority practice Islam,[29] gross domestic product is $136,727 (1st of 185 nations),[30] and is considered to have "very high human development" in the Human Development Index.[31]

In recognition of the challenges of data availability, quality and selection, this paper utilizes a data set collected by one organization (Pew Forum) covering thirty-nine countries comprising more than 38,000 face-to-face

25 CIA: Senegal. www.cia.gov/library/publications/the-world-factbook/geos/sg.html (accessed 31.12.2014); Pew Forum: Muslim Population by Country. http://www.pewforum.org/2011/01/27/table-muslim-population-by-country/ (accessed 31.12.2014).

26 World Bank: GDP per capita, PPP (current international $). http://data.worldbank.org/indicator/NY.GDP.PCAP.PP.CD?order=wbapi_data_value_2013+wbapi_data_value+wbapi_data_value-last&sort=desc (accessed 31.12.2014).

27 World Bank: Poverty headcount ratio at $1.25 a day (PPP) (% of population). http://data.worldbank.org/indicator/SI.POV.DDAY (accessed 31.12.2014).

28 World Bank: Poverty headcount ration at $2 a day (PPP) (% of population). http://data.worldbank.org/indicator/SI.POV.2DAY (accessed 31.12.2014).

29 Pew Forum: Muslim Population by Country. Qatari nationals represent a minority of the population in Qatar, twelve percent of the total population (Jure Snoj: Population of Qatar by Nationality. http://www.bqdoha.com/2013/12/population-qatar (accessed 31.12.2014)). While statistics on religious affiliation are not published by the State of Qatar, the U.S. Department of State also suggests the vast majority of citizens are Muslims (U.S. Department of State: Qatar. http://www.state.gov/j/drl/rls/irf/religiousfreedom/index.htm?year=2013&dlid=222309 (accessed 31.12.2014)).

30 World Bank: GDP per capita, PPP.

31 UNDP: International Human Development Indicators. http://hdr.undp.org/en/statistics/ (accessed 31.12.2014).

interviews, which were conducted in over eighty languages.[32] That data was collected between 2008 and 2012, with countries being surveyed in two groups (2008–2009 and 2011–2012).[33] The data on GDP per capita that is used comes from the World Bank, and is dated to the latter of two years of data collection; for the group of countries surveyed during 2008–2009, financial data from 2009 is used, and for the group of countries surveyed during 2011–2012, financial data from 2012 is used. For the ease of readability in the charts and data that follows, this will hereafter only be indicated in the footnotes. All figures are given in current U.S. dollars, as calculated by the World Bank.

One of the primary limitations in using this data set is the selection criteria of countries that were included, which selected countries wherein more than ten million Muslims lived.[34] For the purposes of this study, which seeks to understand the relationship between economic status and religious adherence, the ideal criteria would have been a survey of countries with a majority Muslim population.[35] In this research, countries with a Muslim population of eighty percent or greater, a significant majority, were selected for analysis. While the eighty percent figure is arbitrary, there was a trend in the data that supported this selection; of the thirty-nine countries surveyed only four countries had Muslim populations between fifty-five and sixty-one percent (Chad, Kazakhstan, Lebanon and Malaysia) and no countries had population percentages from sixty-one to eighty-two percent, thus eighty percent marks the difference between a slight majority and a significant majority. From the thirty-nine countries included in the survey, this amounted to twenty-one countries being included in this study. As a result of the selection criteria, eighteen countries

32 Pew Forum: *The World's Muslims: Religion, Politics and Society*. Washington: Pew Research Center's Forum on Religion & Public Life 2013.

33 Countries surveyed in 2008–2009 were: Djibouti, DR Congo, Nigeria, Uganda, Ethiopia, Mozambique, Kenya, Mali, Ghana, Senegal, Cameroon, Liberia, Chad, Guinea Bissau and Tanzania; Countries surveyed in 2011–2012 were: Russia, Kosovo, Bosnia-Herzegovina, Albania, Kyrgyzstan, Tajikistan, Turkey, Kazakhstan, Azerbaijan, Malaysia, Thailand, Indonesia, Afghanistan, Pakistan, Bangladesh, Iraq, Palestinian Territories, Morocco, Egypt, Jordan, Tunisia, Lebanon, Niger and Uzbekistan (Personal communication with Pew Forum staff).

34 Pew Forum did not include China, India, Saudi Arabia and Syria in their research, which meets their criteria, due to political sensitivities or security concerns.

35 In 2010 this included (from highest percentage to seventy percent): Morocco, Afghanistan, Tunisia, Iran, Western Sahara, Mauritania, Tajikistan, Yemen, Iraq, Jordan, Mayotte, Somalia, Turkey, Azerbaijan, Maldives, Comoros, Niger, Algeria, Palestinian Territories, Saudi Arabia, Djibouti, Libya, Uzbekistan, Pakistan, Senegal, Gambia, Egypt, Turkmenistan, Syria, Mali, Kosovo, Bangladesh, Kyrgyzstan, Indonesia, Oman, Kuwait, Guinea, Albania, Bahrain (Pew Forum: Muslim Population by Country).

that meet the eighty-percent criteria are not included here due to a lack of available data.

As a result of these data limitations, all Muslim-majority countries that are classified as having "very high" human development (Qatar, United Arab Emirates and Bahrain) are not included. This is noteworthy due to their high levels of GDP per capita (1st, 7th and 17th of 185 nations respectively). Other notable Muslim-majority countries that have high levels of GDP per capita and were excluded as a result of available data include Kuwait (GDP per capita 88,259, 3rd of 185) Saudi Arabia (GDP per capita 53,644, 9th of 185) and Oman (GDP per capita 45,797, 13th of 185). For context, all these excluded nations have higher levels of GDP per capita than Australia (18th), Canada (20th), the United Kingdom (24th) and Japan (26th) and have significant (greater than eighty percent) Muslim majorities.

Recognizing these limitations, this study seeks to understand the macro-level quantitative relationship between economic status and religious adherence as it relates to the twenty-one countries analyzed. These findings do not compare religious adherence to other religious communities in other counties, although this would be an interesting future comparative study. The criteria were selected in order to assess the link between economic status and religious adherence using a consistent set of data with a specific set of criteria. This is only one of many potential ways to assess the available data.

Of the many measures, for which data is available, this study looks specifically at two: support for Islamic Law and frequency of prayer. These two measures provide insight into how Muslims feel the wider community ought to be shaped with regard to their religious ideals as well as their actualized practice of the tenants of faith on an individual basis. Other indicators, while relevant to the question at hand, are less useful in terms of analysis. For example, the overwhelming majority of Muslims surveyed throughout the thirty-nine countries affirmed their belief in one God and in the Prophet Muhammad.[36] Of the countries included in this study, over 95 percent made this affirmation.[37] Other areas related to belief were similarly widely accepted throughout all surveyed countries. Praying several times a day is only one manifestation of enacted faith; data on other forms of enacted faith are available and are not analyzed here, such as those who fast during the month of Ramadan

36 Pew Forum: *The World's Muslims: Unity and Diversity*. Washington: Pew Research Center's Forum on Religion & Public Life 2012.

37 Of the 21 countries included in this study, all but Afghanistan was included for this question, resulting in an average of 95.4 percent.

and those who give religious charity (zakāh) annually. The socio-cultural connectivity to fasting during the month of Ramadan and the rulings regarding the requirements of giving charity make these variables more problematic to tie specifically to religious adherence.[38] While prayer can also be a manifestation of socio-cultural norms and/or pressure, this is less likely to influence a practice that is conducted multiple times a day on a regular basis (as opposed to one month a year in fasting and one time per year in charitable giving). Another of the pillars of faith, the pilgrimage (hajj), largely relates to economic ability as much as or more so than religious adherence and/or proximity to Mecca, and was therefore also not included. With the selection of prayer, it is recognized that there are socio-cultural expectations that influence not only practice, but also the way in which answers would be given in a survey. The data collection methodology utilized by Pew Forum was rigorous; however one cannot discount the potential role of these influences in the existing data.

Table 1: GDP per capita and religious adherence

Country	GDP per capita*	% Muslim Population	% Support Islamic Law**	% Pray several times a day
Afghanistan	688	99.8	99	91
Albania	4,406	82.1	12	7
Azerbaijan	7,394	98.4	8	70
Bangladesh	862	90.4	82	39
Djibouti	1,459	97.0	82	77
Egypt	3,256	94.7	74	60
Indonesia	3,551	88.1	72	77
Iraq	6,632	98.9	91	85
Jordan	4,909	98.8	71	68
Kosovo	3,597	91.7	20	41
Kyrgyzstan	1,178	88.8	35	18
Mali	661	92.4	63	81
Morocco	2,900	99.9	83	69
Niger	385	98.3	86	82
Pakistan	1,252	96.4	84	50

38 There is a range of situations wherein a Muslim following Islamic Law needs not to pay the religious charity and therefore not giving this charity is not an indication of lack of religious adherence. For example, there is a minimum amount required that must be held as savings and/or in ownership for a lunar year, after which this charitable giving becomes required. This amount fluctuates with the price of gold, but is currently more than US $3,000.

Palestinian Territories	2,783	97.5	89	74
Senegal	2,242	95.9	55	87
Tajikistan	953	99.0	27	42
Tunisia	4,198	99.8	56	65
Turkey	10,661	98.6	12	42
Uzbekistan	1,719	96.5	***	17

* GDP per capita given according to the latter of the two years during which surveying took place.

** Question stated: "Do you favor or oppose making sharia law, or Islamic law, the official law of the land in our country"? Options of answers were: Favor, Oppose and DK/Ref.

*** This question was not asked by Pew Forum in Uzbekistan and correlations involving this question exclude Uzbekistan.

The Gallup survey data suggests that poverty is correlated positively with valuing religion in day-to-day life. The data analyzed in this study suggests that the correlations are more complex, sometimes in counter-intuitive ways. The first finding is that higher GDP per capita has a weak positive relationship (r=0.136) that is statistically insignificant (p=0.558) with greater percentages of Muslims in the population. The second finding is that higher GDP per capita has a strong negative relationship (r=0.469) that is statistically significant (p=0.037) with support for Islamic Law, in other words as income rises the support for Islamic Law declines. The third finding is that there is no substantial relationship (r=0.068), although statistically insignificant (p=0.771), between higher GDP per capita and higher percentages of people that pray several times per day. The fourth finding is a moderate positive relationship (r=0.323) that is statistically insignificant (p=0.164) between higher percentages of Muslims in the population and greater support for Islamic Law. The fifth finding is a strong positive relationship (r=0.537) that is statistically significant (p=0.012) between higher percentages of Muslims in the population and with higher percentages of people that pray several times per day. The sixth finding is the strongest positive relationship (r=0.624), and is statistically significant (p=0.003), between higher levels of support for Islamic Law and higher percentages of people that pray several times per day.

These correlations, which are not suggested as being causations, present a more complex narrative than the one commonly presented. Rather than lower economic status being associated with religious adherence, there was a weak relationship between higher economic status and a greater proportion of Muslims in the population. Support for Islamic Law significantly declined with a rise in economic status, a finding that may reflect the political sphere as much as it does the individual religious sphere. Nonetheless, the correlation between declining support for Islamic Law and higher GDP per capita is significant. The lack of relationship between higher GDP per capita and higher percentages of the population that pray several times per day is particularly noteworthy. This finding demonstrates that within countries that are religious, in this case countries with significant Muslim-majorities, increases in GDP per capita do not appear to be related to the amount of people that regularly pray several times per day. However, this finding is statistically insignificant and therefore cannot be taken as conclusive. The data also suggests that there are mutually reinforcing interactions between higher percentages of Muslims in the population, support for Islamic Law and higher percentages of people who pray several times per day.

In many countries, including several analyzed here, the Pew Forum also noted that those who prayed more frequently were more likely to favor Islamic Law.[39] This was the case in countries where Muslims were a minority or had a slight majority (as in Russia and Lebanon) and was also the case in countries where Muslims constituted eighty-percent or greater of the population (as in the Palestinian Territories, Tunisia, Kyrgyzstan, Indonesia, Turkey, Bangladesh and Kosovo). Another important sub-factor regarding religious adherence is age. In many surveyed countries the older generation was more adherent to their faith, including with prayer, than the younger generation.[40] One difference that did not exist in the Pew Forum data in all thirty-nine countries was a gendered one. In most surveyed countries, women and men were equally committed to their faith, including with prayer.[41]

Gallup suggested that the point whereby GDP per capita influences religious adherence is US $5,000. In this study, only three of twenty-one countries crossed that threshold. In two of the three (Azerbaijan and Iraq) prayer remained high while GDP per capita exceeding this amount. In the country with the highest GDP per capita (Turkey) prayer was significantly lower. However, these trends ought not be attributed solely to economic status; they are also reflections of regional trends. For example, low levels of support for Islamic Law in Azerbaijan and Turkey also reflect regional trends shared throughout Central Asia, while the high level of support for Islamic Law in Iraq also reflects the regional trend of the Middle East and North Africa,

39 Pew Forum: *The World's Muslims: Religion, Politics and Society.*

40 Pew Forum: *The World's Muslims: Unity and Diversity.*

41 Ibid.

regardless of economic status. Gallup also suggested that US $25,000 was another per capita GDP threshold, after which the importance of religion significantly declines (although the rate remains relatively high after this point, being 44 percent).[42] In this study, no country that passed this threshold, with the lowest GDP per capita being US $385 (Niger) and the highest being US $10,661 (Turkey). The available data limited the countries that were included in this study. Even though they were not included it ought to be noted that there are a number of Muslim-majority countries with very high levels of GDP per capita (Qatar, Kuwait, United Arab Emirates, Saudi Arabia, Oman and Bahrain). It might be mentioned, and correctly so, that most of these nations have small populations, in this regard of note is Saudi Arabia, home to more than thirty million people (for context this is larger than 22 of 28 member states of the European Union).

Poverty and Islam Locally

In 2011, the authors began a qualitative study about cultural change with a community of Muslims living in Cape Town, South Africa, known as Cape Malays. Understanding the dynamics of religious adherence in relation to economic status was not the primary objective of that study, however the in-depth semi-structured interviews provide a wealth of experiential data regarding this link. The original study included twenty-four interviewees (eleven male, thirteen female) from varied socio-economic backgrounds, all of whom were near, or older than, the age of sixty. Participation was voluntary and the interviews were recorded and transcribed, and in some cases translated when interviewees preferred Afrikaans to English. This material is presented in order to provide qualitative data that will complement the quantitative data presented in the previous section. As the objective is to illuminate lived experiences, this section is not meant to be understood as being statistically representative of Muslims in Cape Town, South Africa or the world. Rather, the aim is to provide personal narratives, which enhance and enliven the statistics.

One interviewee, who explained that when she was growing up her family was extremely poor, describes a religious adherence that was tied to living together, a manifestation of societal conviviality, whereby extended family members living in one household was the norm and was one reason for enhanced religious adherence.

42 Crabtree / Pelham: Religion Provides Emotional Boost to World's Poor.

> We were extremely poor but we were ʿibādat [pious] people because we were many people living together in one house. We lived with our grandmother, uncles, aunts and children lived collectively under one roof. We did not have a regular income as far as I can recall and we were generally poor but it was the best years of our lives.[43]

For her, this living together was permanently disrupted by a segregationist policy implemented by the apartheid government, the Group Areas Act, which was first implemented in 1950. This process divided up Muslim communities and families and relocated them; resulting in disconnected social networks, limited access to Islamic schools and mosques and broke apart areas of towns that were predominantly populated by Muslims. The history of Muslims in Cape Town is unique, as a minority ethno-religious group, as they look back on a history of three hundred and fifty years living in the area and living as minorities. As a result of the enforcement of the Group Areas Act, they were forcibly detached from their communities. In this case, it was not a change in wealth that primarily affected religious practice, but government policy.

It is noteworthy that every single interviewee mentioned the negative impacts of the Group Areas Act. However, not all were in agreement that the hardships of the Group Areas Act were the primary causes for changes in religious adherence. One interviewee, who lost a father in her childhood and grew up in a household with limited income, alludes to the link between economic status and social connectivity, in saying: "Society was definitely different. They were there for one another; they helped each other a lot and gave a lot of charity if there was someone poor. We were all poor, but we always had something left for the other."[44] During the lifetime of these interviewees, generally from the 1940s to 2011, GDP per capita has risen dramatically in South Africa. For example, in 1980 GDP per capita (in current US$) was 2,921, in 1990 it rose slightly to 3,182, in 2000 it declined to 3,020, but at the time of the interviews, in 2011, it has dramatically risen to 7,831.[45] The interviewee who links religious adherence to a way of living, mentioned above, felt that the generation of people who have experienced greater wealth and opportunity have lost respect for religion and cannot be compared to the pious people of the past. Although she did not explicitly blame a rise of economic status, the interviewee stated the changes in life are "all about money".

43 Personal communication, 07.08.2011.

44 Personal communication, 05.10.2011.

45 World Bank: GDP per capita (current US$). http://data.worldbank.org/indicator/NY.GDP.PCAP.CD (accessed 31.12.2014).

Another female interviewee similarly suggests the negative changes in religious adherence and family life, but not in a deterministic fashion, rather the changes are a result of the way in which increased wealth is used and the way it influences people.

> If life was a thing money could buy, the rich would live, and the poor would die. Allah in his wisdom made it so that the rich and poor together will go [pass away], so where does this leave the money? That is why I say its money that causes disputes in families because you do not have what I have. You have a better car than what I have so I do not agree with you. What I do not understand is that is what Allah has given you. A car, house, and it breaks the family values it splits it up. What the people do not understand is Allah gives you 10 [South African Rand] then Allah's going to give me 5 but Allah is going to test you with that 10 Allah has given you to see what you going to do with it. Everything is with Allah. Whatever Allah has decreed for you, that is Allah's decree. You cannot change it. Not you or anybody can change it.[46]

It is noteworthy to add that this interviewee, whose aunt embraced Islam and then followed her in that choice later in life, also feels that a rise of economic status has been used positively by some, such as through obtaining greater levels of religious education and through developing more diverse ways of teaching Islam in the form of new curricula and improved teacher training in religious schools. In her experience, wealth is not a primary influence of religious adherence; rather each individual makes choices, some using increased wealth to become more religious while others do not. What is not explored in much of the quantitative data analyses is the rise of religious adherence, particularly as greater economic status has provided the means (both in terms of time as well as access) to gain religious knowledge. Turkey may be an example of a nation that has experienced significant rises in GDP per capita as well as an increase in religious adherence, although this point is debated and some of these changes may reflect politics more than individual practice.[47] A much more detailed study is required in order to answer this question conclusively.

Another member of the community, whose father immigrated from Zimbabwe and mother from the United Kingdom, suggests that the piety of the past was simplistic, and that the religious education and depth of religious knowledge was limited. New economic opportunity not only enhanced

46 Personal communication, 07.08.2011.

47 Anand Giridharadas: In Turkey, Forging a New Identity. http://www.nytimes.com/2012/12/01/world/europe/01iht-currents01.html?pagewanted=all&_r=1& (accessed 04.01.2015); Barry Rubin: Turkey Trots toward Islamism. http://www.jpost.com/Opinion/Columnists/The-Region-Turkey-trots-toward-Islamism (accessed 04.01.2015).

knowledge and education, but she feels, it also improved the practice of many, giving the example of the modest attire of women. At the same time, however, this interviewee feels some societal values have declined, such as respect for religious practices, a decline that is not restricted to the Muslim community, but felt throughout the whole society.

Not all agree, however, some feel changes in economic status have direct impacts on the way religious traditions are valued. One female interviewee, who says she was raised in poverty and had a father who regularly read the Qur'an and taught it to children in the neighborhood, feels that way. Unlike the experience above, this interviewee feels that the attire of Muslim women has declined in its modesty, with people now dressing "half naked", attributing the cause of these changes to an increase in economic status:

> At the end of the day it's about money. If you have too much money, I will not look at you and you cannot look at me. Back then it was not so. People helped each other. People came and knocked on my father's door. Sometimes we never had [money]. My father would send me to the Indian shop to get a *kroon* [the previous currency denomination that would be equivalent to today's one rand (1 ZAR)] and write it on the book. Then my father would give the woman a half *kroon*. Today they chase you away. There is no help today. People tell you straight away they cannot help you.[48]

These personal narratives and lived experiences express a number of trends that ought to be better encapsulated within quantitative national-level statistical analyses. Amidst economic change, there are diverse arrays of responses, many of which have unique causes to consider. In this case, legislation that forced the relocation of individuals may have caused greater changes to religious adherence than the rise of economic status. Due to a lack of studies conducted over time, this specific question is difficult to answer, however future research should make an effort to assess religious adherence over time. Greater contextualization of this nature may enable improved understanding of when, why and how economic change does and does not play a primary role in influencing religious adherence. Religious adherence may improve as a result of enhanced economic status, such as through improved educational opportunities, educational training, curricula and awareness raising activities using new technologies. This may not be the case for all people, as demonstrated within these narratives, but it suggests that the statistical data may not reflect the dynamic nature of religious adherence when correlating it to economic status. Anirudh Krishna's research on poverty enabled entirely new avenues of understanding macro-level data on poverty, such that statistics are

48 Personal communication, 22.06.2011.

not thought to represent a static body of people but represent a dynamic and constantly changing body.[49] The quantitative figure may be relatively stable, but the individuals included and excluded are in flux. The research presented here does not provide sufficient evidence to state that religious adherence operates in a similar fashion, however the qualitative data demonstrates that much more research is needed in order to better understand the dynamics and details of quantitative data.

Conclusion

The theological context suggests that much more nuanced and deconstructed discussions are needed with regard to what poverty is, how it is measured and the way in which theological knowledge might contribute to the understanding of trends in religious adherence in relation to economic status. The quantitative data demonstrated that the generalized trends might be correct in some cases, such as declining support for Islamic Law with increasing economic status, but not in all cases, such as the lack of correlation between rising economic status and regular daily prayer. These findings show that economic status affects religious practices in unique ways. Much more data and research is required in order to better understand these dynamics. The qualitative data outlined the diverse experiences individuals have with economic status in relation to religious adherence. This section highlighted two important points: (1) the need for greater contextualization of national-level statistical data to avoid justifying assumptions through correlations without assessing the range of factors involved, and (2) the need for improved understanding of religious adherence that explores the dynamics of increases and decreases within a population and between religious practices, which may not appear within national-level data.

In an interview with the Canadian Broadcasting Corporation, Marcus Noland, a senior fellow at the Peterson Institute of International Economics, stated that analyses about economic status and religious adherence are a "more complex psychological and social phenomenon than just looking at a snapshot of cross-state data or even cross-income data and saying religion either keeps you poor or not being religious gets you rich."[50] It is on this note that this

49 Anirudh Krishna: *One Illness Away: Why People Become Poor and How They Escape Poverty*. New York: Oxford UP 2010.

50 Kazi Stastna: Do Countries Lose Religion as They Gain Wealth? http://www.cbc.ca/news/world/do-countries-lose-religion-as-they-gain-wealth-1.1310451 (accessed 31.12.2014).

paper also concludes; the relationship between economic status and religious adherence is complex and these findings suggest that the impact of changing economic status is diverse, not only affecting individuals differently but also impacting various manifestations of religious adherence in unique ways.

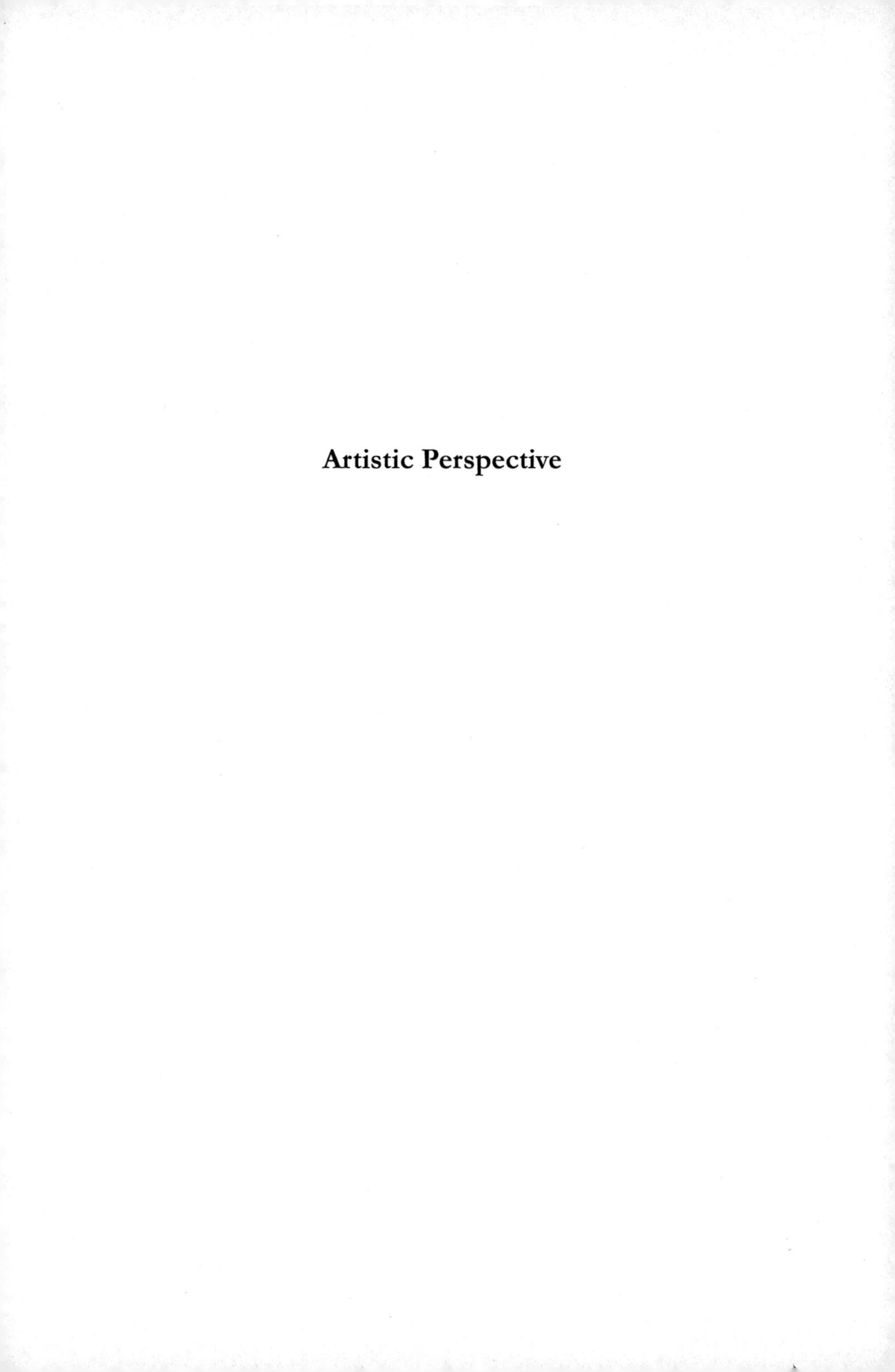

Artistic Perspective

Giobbe il Povero

A Social Reading of Giovanni Bellini's Sacred Allegory

Atara Moscovich

"Iconographical meaning in Bellini's painting is rich, elusive and inexhaustible"[1], wrote Norman Land, referring to one of the most enigmatic and fascinating paintings in art history, Giovanni Bellini's (1435–1518) painting, *The Sacred Allegory* (Fig. 1, ca. 1490–1510). This work has attracted much scholarly attention and was subject to a wide range of interpretations. Oscar Bätschmann commented: "Bellini's *Sacred Allegory* belongs to a group of works that refuse to be decoded, and which thereby continually generate new readings"[2]. The aim of the current paper is to suggest a new reading of this painting, related to the socio-economic conditions in Venice in the late 15th and early 16th centuries. However, since I concur with Bätschmann's position that the painting has multiple readings, I maintain that an inclusive interpretation of the work is not possible. Thus, the reading suggested in this paper constitutes only one possibility among many others.

Giovanni Bellini's painting *The Sacred Allegory* is a horizontal, rectangular painting featuring a group of people on a terrace, on the shore of a body of water – a river or a canal. The identities of some of the figures depicted are ambiguous, and will be discussed below in detail. A white parapet surrounds the terrace. In the center of the parapet is a gate leading to the body of water, and behind it are several barren trees. The terrace is paved with colored marble; the dark paving stones create the shape of a cross. In the middle of the cross is a small pot with a small tree bearing silver fruit. Like the human figures, the fruit is also ambiguous; some authors having interpreted them as apples, with others seeing them as oranges.[3] Four infants are playing around

The author would like to thank Professor Simona Cohen from Tel Aviv University for supervising the MA thesis on which this paper is based, and for reviewing an earlier draft of this paper.

1 Norman E. Land: On the Poetry of Giovanni Bellini's 'Sacred Allegory'. In: *Artibus et historiae* 5,10 (1984), pp. 61–66, here p. 64.

2 Oskar Bätschmann: *Giovanni Bellini*. London: Reaktion 2008, p. 131.

3 The tree was already connected to the issue of charity by Susan J. Delaney: The Iconography of Bellini's Sacred Allegory. In: *Art Bulletin* 15, 3 (1977), pp. 331–335. However, she reads charity as a religious virtue and does not relate it to the socio-economic conditions in Venice at

the tree, three of them are naked and one is clothed. Most authors interpret the clothed child as Christ.

In addition, the painting depicts several other groups of people: Job and St. Sebastian are pictured on the right, with three figures given behind the parapet and three women on the left. Job and St. Sebastian appear naked except for loincloths according to their traditional iconography, and resemble their design in a previous painting by Bellini, *San Giobbe Altarpiece*, ordered for the Church of San Giobbe in Venice. St. Sebastian's hands are tied behind his back, and Job is in a praying posture. Almost all the other adult figures are depicted praying, facing Christ the Child. Among these figures is a bearded, white-haired man leaning on the parapet, three women – one of whom is sitting on a throne and usually identified as Virgin Mary – and two additional men behind the parapet – one of whom is holding a scroll and a sword, and the other, wearing a white turban, is turned away as if he intends to leave the painted space. On the river's opposite bank, an encounter between a monk and a centaur is represented.

There is no knowledge regarding the commission of the painting, nor of its original intended site of display. The horizontal composition and size of the painting suggest that it was commissioned for a private home.[4] The fact that the painting offers several points of focus would support this assumption, as it suggests that the work was conceived under the expectation that the viewer would be allowed a close examination of its details, a proximity of attention not usually possible within a church setting. However, its possible intended domestic display does not exclude the strong communal and local societal emphasis implied within the painting.

The dating of this work remains complicated and undetermined, and according to various authors, ranges from the 1470s to the first years of the

that period. See also another interpretation of the tree in Stefano Coltellaci / Marco Lattanzi: Proposte Iconilogiche per la Sacra Allegoria degli Uffizi. In: *Giorgione e la Cultura Veneta tra '400 e '500: Mito, Allegoria, Analisi Iconologica.* Rome: Istituto de Storia dell'Arte Università di Roma 1981, pp. 59–79, here pp. 65–70.

4 See also Heidi J. Hornik: The Venetian Images by Bellini and Carpaccio: Job as Intercessor or Prophet? In: *Review & Expositor* 99,4 (2002), pp. 541–568, here p. 548. The format of the altarpieces in Venice was usually vertical, see Peter Humfrey: *The Altarpiece in Renaissance Venice.* New Haven: Yale UP 1993, passim. On religious paintings in private homes in Venice, see Patricia Fortini Brown: Behind the Walls: The Material Culture of Venetian Elites. In: John Martin / Dennis Romano (eds): *Venice Reconsidered: The History and Civilization of an Italian City-State, 1297–1797.* Baltimore: Johns Hopkins UP 2000, pp. 295–338, here pp. 308–310, 321; Ronda Kasl: Holy Households: Art and Devotion in Renaissance Venice. In: Ead. (ed.): *Giovanni Bellini and the Art of Devotion.* Indianapolis: Indianapolis Museum of Art 2004, pp. 58–89, here pp. 79–82.

Fig. 1: Giovanni Bellini: *Sacred Allegory*, ca. 1490–1500, oil and tempera on wood, 73 x 119 cm, Florence, Galleria degli Uffizi.

16th century.[5] This painting is one of several artworks created in Venice in the late 15th and early 16th century which feature the figure of Job. The other artworks are: *Job and St. Francis* (ca. 1471), a marble relief by Pietro Lombardo (1435–1515) above the entrance to San Giobbe Church, Giovanni Bellini's *San Giobbe Altarpiece*[6], Vittore Carpaccio's (1464–1525/6) *Meditation on the Passion*[7],

5 For a review of dating by the various authors, see Anchise Tempestini: *Giovanni Bellini*. Paris: Gallimard 1999, p. 152. Some authors (among them Samuel Terrien: *The Iconography of Job through the Centuries: Artists as Biblical Interpreters*. University Park, PA: Pennsylvania State Press 1996, pp. 132, 135; Tempestini: *Giovanni Bellini*, p. 153; Keith Christiansen: Giovanni Bellini and the Practice of Devotional Painting. In: Kasl (ed.): *Giovanni Bellini and the Art of Devotion*, pp. 6–57, here p. 44; Bätschmann: *Giovanni Bellini*, pp. 133–134) tried to connect the *Sacred Allegory* with the patroness and art collector, the Duchess Isabela d'Este's attempt to commission a painting from Bellini. Her attempt is documented in a correspondence, quoted in the above-mentioned papers, between her and the poet Pietro Bembo, who served as an intermediary between her and the artist, yet there is no proof that the *Sacred Allegory* was the painting discussed in this correspondence.

6 471 x 86.7 cm, oil and tempera on wood, 1475–1487, Venice, Galleria del'Accademia.

7 86.7 x 70.5 cm, oil and tempera on wood, ca. 1490–1510, New York, Metropolitan Museum of Art.

Vittore Carpaccio's *Dead Christ*[8], and Marcello Fogolino's (1470/1488?–1548): *The Virgin with St. Job and St. Gottardo*[9].

Two of the most obvious characteristics that almost all of these artworks share (with the exception of Fogolino's painting) are: 1) that Job is figured without the lesions, which are his traditional attribute, and 2) that he is surrounded by other figures, thus represented as part of a community,[10] which contradicts the Biblical text, where Job laments his loneliness and feels especially humiliated because of his exclusion from his community.[11] Further, there are formal elements in these artworks that point to his belonging to this community; he shares the same space as the other figures, his scale and his modeling are equivalent to those of the other figures.

The exceptional representation of Job in these artworks precipitated two assumptions. The first is that these works do not refer to Job as a plague saint – or at least, not *only* as a plague saint. The second assumption is that an interpretation of these works should be a social one. And, the occurrence of the figure of Job in such a prominent body of artworks in Venice in such a short period would lead to the assumption that this social interpretation would have a unique local meaning. A fact that might lend support to this assumption is that at the very same period, in 1494, Girolamo Savonarola delivered for forty consecutive days sermons about the *Book of Job* in Florence,[12] and yet, in spite of Savonarola's immense influence on Florentine culture, no such presence of the figure of Job can be found in Florentine art.

Methodology

The idea of multiple interpretations stems from the Christian method used in reading the Holy Scriptures, a method in which each text and each character held multiple meanings – literal, allegorical, moral and anagogical – which may even, at times, contradict each other.[13] As a Biblical figure, Job was

8 185 x 145 cm., tempera on wood, ca. 1510–1520, Berlin, Staatliche Museen, Gemäldegalerie.

9 203 x 160 cm., oil on wood, ca. 1508, Milan, Galleria di Brera.

10 Hornik: The Venetian Images, p. 554.

11 This feeling of loneliness is referred to, for example, in the following verses: Job 16:7–11; 19:13–19; 30:1; 30:3; 30:8–14. The following papers have raised my awareness to the importance of Job's solitude: René Girard: The Ancient Trail Trodden by the Wicked: Job as Scapegoat. In: *Semeia* 33 (1985), pp. 13–41; Alec Basson: Just Skin and Bones: Longing for Wholeness of the Body in the *Book of Job*. In: *Vetus testamentum* 58,3 (2008), pp. 287–299.

12 The lectures are compiled in Girolamo Savonarola: *Prediche Sopra Giobbe*. Roma: Belardetti 1957.

13 Beryl Smalley: *The Study of the Bible in the Middle Ages*. Notre Dame, IN: University of Notre Dame Press 1964, passim.

interpreted, among other interpretations, in addition to the ones discussed here, as a pre-figuration of Christ, as a symbol of the Church, and as a symbol of virtues such as patience or fortitude.[14]

An additional methodological approach applied in this research is the use, wherever possible, of such primary sources (books and visual material) as might have been available to Bellini or to his clients. One could assume with a great amount of confidence that interpretations of Job represented in this work were influenced by the book *Moralia in Iob* by St. Gregory the Great (540–604), published in Venice in two editions, in 1480 and in 1494.[15] Throughout this book, St. Gregory the Great employs the multi-dimensional system of interpretation, and thus, this book must have contributed to the perception of Job as a figure that can have a wide range of meanings simultaneously.

A further justification for the multi-dimensional reading of Bellini's painting can be derived by noting an additional unique feature of this work: like Job, who is depicted without his characteristic wounds, the other figures are also represented without their usual attributes, such as St. Peter without his keys, and St. Mary Magdalene without the oil pitcher. The depiction of these characters as stripped of their attributes makes their identification less clear, and thus renders the figures open to multiple interpretations.[16]

Below, I attempt an identification of these figures, in order to line out parallel aspects between these characters and the figure of Job, aspects that enhance the social meaning. My attempts to identify these figures drew largely from a primary source for the biographies of saints, *The Golden Legend* by Jacobus de Voragine, which was written in 1260 and was widespread in Europe, including an Italian version, published in Venice in 1475.[17] These attempts to identify the figures represented in this work – and the implications of this

14 Jennifer O'Reilly: *Studies in the Iconography of Virtues and Vices in the Middle Ages.* New York: Garland 1988, pp. 285–303. See also a double interpretation of Job – both as a prophet and an intercessor – in the Venetian paintings of this period, including *The Sacred Allegory*, in Hornik: The Venetian Images.

15 Frederick Hartt: Carpaccio's Meditation on the Passion of Christ. In: *Art Bulletin* 22,1 (1940), pp. 25–35, here pp. 29–30. In addition, the book was also available in manuscripts at a much earlier date, such as the manuscript *Cod. Lat. Z. 24*, probably written in the San Ferdiano monastery in Pisa in the 13th century, and which was included in Bessarion's donation to the Biblioteca Marciana, see Marino Zorzi (ed.): *Biblioteca Marciana Venezia.* Firenze: Nardini 1999, p. 76.

16 Augusto Gentili: Bellini and Landscape. In: Peter Humfrey (ed.): *The Cambridge Companion to Giovanni Bellini.* New York: Cambridge UP 2004, pp. 167–181, here p. 174.

17 Terisio Pignatti: *Carpaccio: La Leggenda di Sant'Orsola.* Firenze: SADEA / Sansoni 1965, p. [2].

identification – support the interpretation of the *Sacred Allegory* suggested in the current paper.

An additional primary source that was used is *The Testament of Job*, an apocryphal book written probably in Aramaic around 100 BC–100 AD and ascribed to Jewish sources.[18] Visual sources employed refer to the Byzantine illustrated manuscripts of the *Book of Job* from the Middle Ages, many of which were available in Italy (especially in Venice) during the period in which *Sacred Allegory* was painted.[19]

Literary Review

As mentioned above, there were numerous attempts to interpret the meaning of Bellini's *Sacred Allegory*. Some authors regarded it as a depiction of Paradise,[20] or a paradise that is also simultaneously a reflection of our own world.[21] Others read it as an illustration of the 14th century poem *Le Pélegrinage de l'Âme* by Guillaume de Deguilleville;[22] as an illustration of the verse "Mercy and truth are met together; righteousness and peace have kissed each other. Truth shall spring out of earth; and righteousness shall look down from heaven" (Psalms, 85:10–11);[23] or as a complicated Christian allegory, referring to the dispute between God's sons in the Hebrew Midrash based on this verse.[24] Other readings saw the work as a lyrical image of the Church, to which the saints offered their pleas during

18 *Testament of Job*, transl. from Greek by M. R. James. Cambridge: Cambridge UP 1897. See also Kathi Meyer: St. Job as a Patron of Music. In: *Art Bulletin* 36,1 (1954), pp. 21–31, here p. 23; William Gruen: Seeking a Context for the Testament of Job. In: *Journal for the Study of the Pseudepigrapha* 18,3 (2009), pp. 163–179. As for the Jewish sources of the *Testament of Job*, see also: Annette Yoshiko Reed: Job as Jobab: The Interpretation of Job in LXX JOB 42:17b–e. In: *Journal of Biblical Literature* 120,1 (2001), pp. 31–55, here pp. 51–52.

19 Most of the illuminations are found in Stella Papadaki-Oekland: *Byzantine Illuminated Manuscripts of the Book of Job: A Preliminary Study of the Miniature Illustration, its Origin and Development.* Athens: Brepols 2009. As to Bellini's interest in the Byzantine art, see David Rosand: Review of *Giovanni Bellini* by G. Robertson. In: *Art Quarterly* 33 (1970), pp. 72–74, here p. 74.

20 Wolfgang Braunfels: Giovanni Bellinis 'Paradiesgartlein'. In: *Das Münster* 9 (1956), pp. 1–13.

21 Johannes Wilde: *Venetian Art from Bellini to Titian.* Oxford: Clarendon 1974, p. 40.

22 Gustav Ludwig: Giovanni Bellinis sogenannte Madonna am See in den Uffizien, eine religiöse Allegorie. In: *Jarbuch der Königlich Preussischen Kunstsammlungen* 22 (1902), pp. 163–186.

23 Philippe Verdier: L'allegoria della Misericordia e della Giustizia di Giambellino agli Uffizi. In: *Atti dell'Instituto Veneto di Scienze, Lettere e Arti* 111 (1952–1953), pp. 97–116, here pp. 102–103; Delaney: The Iconography, pp. 332–334.

24 Verdier: L'allegoria, p. 102.

the plague;[25] or as a plea of Job, St. Sebastian and St. Mary Magdalene in favor of the persecuted homosexuals and prostitutes;[26] and contrasting conception – that of the painting as an expression of the spiritual life that flourished in Venice at the time;[27] as a *Sacra Conversazione* arranged in a different spatial array;[28] as a painting encompassing nativity, death and eternal life, in which the main subject is lyrical meditation;[29] as meditation on the Passion;[30] as meditation on the Incarnation;[31] or as a painting intended to evoke thought.[32] Here, we see a myriad of interpretations, each profound and interesting, and each contributing to an understanding of the multiple layers of the painting. However, none of these cited interpretations (except for a partial explanation in Samuel Terrien's interpretation) offered a reading based on socio-economic conditions of the period, and this is what I will attempt to do in this paper.

Job and the Venetian Solidarity

A. 'Father to the Poor'

I would like to provide support for the reading I offer here by reviewing the social conditions in Venice during the pertinent period. As mentioned above, the reason I was looking for a social meaning can be found in an aspect characterizing this artwork (as well as the other ones describing Job in Venice during this period), and that is – Job is depicted as part of a community.
Here, I would like to try to define some characteristics of this community: The Venetian community of this period was characterized by a high level of solidarity, which was expressed in unique organizational structures – namely, the *scuole* (singular: *scuola*), which were voluntary, charitable confraternities established with the support and approval of the government from the

25 Delaney: The Iconography, p. 335. Because of St. Sebastian's presence, many authors connected the painting to the plague. However, this issue will not be discussed here, since the plague could be another line, or stratum, of interpretation.

26 Terrien: *The Iconography of Job*, pp. 127–135.

27 Coltellaci / Lattanzi: Studi Belliniani, pp. 59–79.

28 Nicolò Rasmo: La Sacra Conversazione Belliniana degli Uffizi e il problema della sua comprensione. In: *Carro Minore* 5/6 (1946), pp. 229–240.

29 Land: On the Poetry, pp. 61–66.

30 Rona Goffen: *Giovanni Bellini*. New Haven: Yale UP 1989, p. 117.

31 Giles Robertson: *Giovanni Bellini*. Oxford: Clarendon 1968, p. 101.

32 Christiansen: Practice of Devotional Painting, p. 49; Gentili: Bellini and Landscape, pp. 175–176; Bätschmann: *Giovanni Bellini*, p. 138.

13th century onward.[33] They were constituted by people from various social classes, and provided for the needs of their members in a system of mutual assistance according to the problems encountered – loans, donations, residence, dowries, funerals etc. The charity of the confraternities was closely linked to religion – each of the confraternities was dedicated to a saint or a religious concept such as charity or mercy – and their charitable work was done for the sake of God. The scope of the activity of the *scuole* was unique to Venice. In June 1521, 120 *scuole piccole* (small *scuole*, in addition to the five large ones) were documented at the funeral procession of the Doge.[34]

Bellini, as a native Venetian, was undoubtedly aware of this activity, and was an active participant in it. He was a member of the *Scuola Grande di San Marco*, one of the most important *scuole*. Furthermore, Bellini served as a deacon in this *scuola*, and in this capacity, he was charged with handling the applications of the poor for support. He is documented as a member in 1484 and as a deacon in 1486 and 1489,[35] which is earlier than the usually presumed date of *The Sacred Allegory*.

At this point, I would argue that Job could represent the wealthy citizens of the city, and thus serve as a reminder that they should provide for the poor. To support this argument, I would like to turn to the beginning of the *Book of Job*, where the description of his wealth ends with the words: "so that this man was the greatest of all the men of the east" (Job, 1:3). Later, Job calls for witnesses to speak of his treatment of the poor:

> I was eyes to the blind, and feet was I to the lame.
> I was a father to the poor:
> And the cause which I knew not I searched out.
> And I brake the jaws of the wicked,
> and plucked the spoil out of his teeth (Job, 29: 15–17).

One of the characteristics Job shares with the other figures in the *Sacred Allegory* is the relinquishing of property in favor of the poor. On the left side of the painting is a group of women whose interpretation is usually disputed, with the exception being the middle figure (the woman on the throne) who is usually assumed to be Virgin Mary. The other two women are interpreted as either Virtues or as saints.

33 Brian Pullan: *Rich and Poor in Renaissance Venice.* Cambridge, MA: Harvard UP 1971, passim.

34 Ibid., pp. 33–34.

35 Goffen: *Giovanni Bellini*, pp. 260, 264.

Using the method of multi-dimensional interpretation, it might be possible to see these women as Virtues, and I shall refer to this notion later. However, according to an interpretation that views these figures as saints, the 'hovering' of the left female figure would support a reading seeing that woman as St. Mary Magdalene.[36] The *Golden Legend* tells that St. Maximus "saw the blessed Mary Magdalene standing in the quire or choir yet among the angels that brought her, and was lift up from the earth the space of two or three cubits".[37] Another story from the *Golden Legend* connects Mary Magdalene with the concept of charity: Mary Magdalene, her sister Martha and her brother Lazarus were very wealthy, and subsequently sold their property and gave the money to Christ's apostles.[38]

In an attempt to identify the second female figure wearing a crown as another saint, authors sought to interpret her as one of the virgin martyrs – St. Ursula, St. Catherina, or St. Lucy[39] – all of whom are often depicted in art as wearing crowns. In the present context, interpreting this woman as St. Lucy seems the most appropriate. Once again, in the *Golden Legend* we are told that St. Lucy sold all of her property and gave that money to the poor, and we are also told that when the judge orders her to make a sacrifice to the idols, she replies: "Sacrifice which pleaseth God is to visit the widows and orphans, and to help them in their need: I have not ceased these three years past to make to God such sacrifice."[40]

Another saint depicted in the picture is St. Anthony Abbot, who appears in the painting's background, and could be identified according to the legend of his encounter with a centaur.[41] The *Golden Legend* also attributes a story to

36 See literary review on the issue of her (missing?) feet in Tempestini: *Giovanni Bellini*, p. 152; Coltellaci / Lattanzi: Studi Belliniani, pp. 73–74.

37 Jacobus de Voragine: *The Golden Legend or Lives of the Saints*, 1275. First Edition Published 1470, 1483. Transl. from Latin by William Caxton. Edinburgh: Edinburgh UP 1900 (reprinted 1922, 1931) http://www.fordham.edu/halsall/basis/goldenlegend/ (accessed 20.04.2015), vol. 4, pp. 36–42. (Since the website from which the excerpts of *The Golden Legend* were taken does not state the exact pages the excerpts appear on, rather only the first page of every chapter, here – and in all the footnotes referring to *The Golden Legend* – all the pages of the chapter from which the excerpt was taken shall be noted).

38 Ibid.

39 Goffen: *Giovanni Bellini*, p. 116.

40 Voragine: *Golden Legend*, vol. 2, pp. 59–61.

41 I located the text in another version of the *Golden Legend*: *The Golden Legend of Jacobus de Voragine*, vol. 2, transl. from Latin by Granger Ryan / Helmut Ripperger. Salem, NH: Ayer 1987, p. 89. The monk was probably identified for the first time as St. Anthony Abbot by Verdier: L'allegoria della Misericordia, p. 114.

St. Anthony Abbott, in which he sells all his property and gives the money to the poor.[42]

Thus, it becomes evident that one of the common characteristics shared by the community of saints depicted here is their charitable support for the poor. Therefore, one might say that the saints in the picture offer a reflection of Venetian society, characterized as it was by solidarity, strong social awareness and care for its less fortunate members. In addition, I would suggest that Job, and certain other saints who are depicted here, do not only represent the benefactors, but rather also the recipients of charity.

B. *Giobbe il Povero*

Brian Pullan refers to two groups of poor people integral to the Venetian community of this period and considered as worthy of charity: the 'worthy poor' (*poveri meritavoli*) and the 'ashamed poor' (*poveri vergognosi*).[43] The 'worthy poor' were decent citizens, worthy of charity due to their honest behavior. The 'ashamed poor' were impoverished nobles, who were too ashamed to apply for charity. Job was a figure both groups could identify with. First, Job could represent the 'ashamed poor'. Here, I would refer back to the already-quoted verse, which describes him as the richest person in the East (Job, 1:3), who subsequently and quite suddenly lost all of his property (Job, 1:13–17). There is also an iconographic tradition of depicting Job as a king,[44] which emphasizes his noble origin. This tradition is likely based on the verse "and dwelt as a king in the army" (Job, 29:25), and perhaps on the apocryphal book *The Testament of Job*, in which he is explicitly referred to as a king.[45]

Secondly, Job could represent the 'worthy poor', according to his description in the Biblical text: "and that man was perfect and upright, and one that feared God, and eschewed evil" (Job, 1:1). Those epithets were not ascribed to any other protagonist in the Bible, not even to the Bible's greatest figures. We should bear in mind that the Bible is objective even towards patriarchs such as Jacob, or the kings Saul and David, and does not censor the negative aspects of their characters and deeds. Thus, for example, we are even told

42 Voragine: *Golden Legend* (as in fn. 31. From here forward all the citation are taken from this version), vol. 2, pp. 100–103. http://legacy.fordham.edu/halsall/basis/goldenlegend (accessed 20.04.2015).

43 Pullan: *Rich and Poor*, pp. 107, 239, 269, 400.

44 Terrien: *The Iconography of Job*, pp. 45–49, 82; Papadaki-Oekland: *Illuminated Manuscripts*, pp. 43–47; Laura Carnevale: *Giobbe dall'Antichità al Medioeveo: Testi, Tradizioni, Immagini*. Bari: Edigpuglia 2010, pp. 146–148.

45 *Testament of Job*, 1:13.

that, "Noah was a just man and perfect in his generations" (Genesis, 6:9), and the exegesis to this verse maintains that Noah was a righteous man relatively to his generation, but not an absolutely righteous man.[46]
In addition, the Biblical text is usually concise, and the verse describing Job demonstrates an opposite tendency, of redundant wording, a tendency that is expressed in four different epithets: 'perfect', 'upright', 'one that feared God', and 'eschewed evil'. Later in the same chapter, this redundant wording is repeated exactly: "a perfect and an upright man, one that feareth God, and escheweth evil" (Job, 1:8). This repetition enhances Job's uniqueness, especially since God himself says these words, emphasizing, "there is none like him in the earth" (Job, 1:8).
This interpretation is further supported upon returning to an analysis of the figures surrounding Job in the *Sacred Allegory*, wherein one finds a parallel between Job's chastity and the chastity of the other figures depicted. The infants, obviously innocent, are interpreted by some authors as the first martyrs – the babies murdered in the Massacre of the Innocents[47] – and consequently their reading as pure figures is enhanced. This explanation also applies if we accept their interpretation as the pure or redeemed souls in paradise.[48] In addition, the woman on the throne is usually interpreted as Virgin Mary, the purest figure in Christian tradition. The female saint depicted wearing the crown – whether read as Ursula, Catherina or Lucy, all of whom were virgin martyrs that chose death over the violation of their chastity – also appears as a symbol of chastity and virtue.
However, as mentioned earlier, some authors have suggested that the 'hovering' figure represented is that of St. Mary Magdalene. This interpretation leads us to the next argument, according to which Job does not only represent the normative poor – who were integral to society – but, together with St. Mary Magdalene and St. Sebastian, he also represents the aberrant, the marginal, the strangers and wanderers.
Brian Pullan indicates a change in the Venetian perception of charity in the 15th and 16th centuries. This change manifested as an enhanced awareness to

46 See Rashi's (1040–1115) exegesis of this verse, in *Mikra'ot Gedolot*. Venice: Daniel Bomberg 1524–1526 (in Hebrew): http://he.wikisource.org/wiki/%D7%9E%22%D7%92_%D7%91%D7%A8%D7%90%D7%A9%D7%99%D7%AA_%D7%95_%D7%98 (accessed 20.04.2015).

47 See literary reviews in Tempestini: *Giovanni Bellini*, p. 152; Coltellaci / Lattanzi: Studi Belliniani, pp. 59–62.

48 Robertson: *Giovanni Bellini*, p. 101.

poverty, and a willingness to take responsibility – not only for the aforementioned groups of the normative poor to which the *scuole* already catered, but also for the aberrant and the outcasts, those who lacked familial or communal safety networks.[49] Thus, for example, in the 1470s temporary shelters were built for the vagabonds, and the government allowed the *scuole* to impart charity to people who were not necessarily members of the *scuole*.[50]

As stated earlier, Job is often described in Biblical texts as feeling like an outcast and a stranger. Such feelings might then make him a suitable figure to represent the strangers and the marginal members of society. Again, employing the comparison across the characteristics of those figures presented in this painting, we see that Job appears to share feelings of humiliation with the other saints depicted in this painting. First and foremost, he shares this feeling with St. Paul, who also suffered scorn and humiliation.[51] St. John Chrysostom (347–407) wrote a comparison between Job and St. Paul dating back to the 4th century.[52] As the full text of this comparison is quoted in the *Golden Legend*, it was likely to have been well known in the 15th century. Among other characteristics, Chrysostom makes a case for the scorn and humiliation: "Which not of three or four friends, but of all men and of his brethren he suffered opprobrium, and was confused and cursed of them all, and he took everything meekly and patiently"[53].

It should be noted here that St. Gregory the Great compares Job's sons to Christ's apostles, and furthermore, wherein he interprets Job as a prefiguration of Christ, he interprets Job's sons as a prefiguration of the apostles.[54] This creates an additional symbolic link between the figures of St. Peter, St. Paul and the figure of Job, given that according to St. Gregory the Great's

49 Pullan: *Rich and Poor*, p. 216.

50 Ibid., pp. 212–213, 280.

51 The person behind the parapet that carries the scroll and the sword is interpreted as St. Paul, and since the SS. Peter and Paul are usually represented in art together, most of the interpretations see these figures as SS. Peter and Paul. For other interpretations for these figures, see Giovanni Battista Cavalcaselle / Joseph Archer Crowe: *A History of Painting in North Italy*. New York: AMS 1912, vol. 3, pp. 6–7; Rasmo: La Sacra Conversazione, pp. 229–240; Gentili: Bellini and Landscape, p. 174; Verdier: L'allegoria della Misericordia, p. 110.

52 Voragine: *Golden Legend*, vol. 4, pp. 15–22 http://www.fordham.edu/halsall/basis/goldenlegend (accessed 20.04.2015).

53 Ibid.

54 Saint Gregorius the Great: *Moralia in Job*, transl. from Latin by John Henry Parker. London: Oxford, Parker & Rivington 1844, book I, xiv, p. 19. http://www.lectionarycentral.com/GregoryMoraliaIndex.html (accessed 20.04.2015).

conception, these saintly figures can be interpreted both as Christ's apostles and as Job's sons.

A reference to Job's sons can be found also in other figures in Bellini's painting. Here, I would maintain that the infants depicted in the *Sacred Allegory* can also be read as a reference to Job's sons. Job looks towards them in the image, and they are placed on the main axis of the cross of the marble floor on which Job is also placed.[55] Further, Job appears to pray for them – and Job used to burn offerings and pray on behalf of his sons (Job, 1:5). Here, a certain amount of reservation is required, since almost all the figures in the painting appear to be praying. However, when examining the Byzantine illuminated manuscripts of the *Book of Job*, we shall see that Job is depicted in a position of prayer on those pages that illustrate his receiving the terrible news of his sons' death.[56]

Here, we should ask whether a connection exists between Job's children and charity. We might seek the answer to this question by turning to Job's daughters. As we have established, there are a myriad possible readings of the figures of the women on the left of the image – one of which being that these women exist as figural personifications of Virtues.

According to this reading, the figure with the crown is often interpreted as 'Truth', and the other as 'Righteousness', according to the verse "Truth shall spring out of earth; and righteousness shall look down from heaven" (Psalms, 85:11).[57] This interpretation is drawn from the apparent figuring of the woman wearing a crown as kneeling (as a matter of fact, her height is identical to the other female figure, hence she cannot be said to be kneeling), and the other woman's appearance of hovering. This 'hovering' has caused some to interpret her as a personification of 'Hope'.[58]

This analysis appears to be supported when we read that St. Gregory the Great interpreted the names of Job's daughters – Jemima (Dies), Kezia (Casia) and Kerenhappuch (Conustibii) – as allegories of the Virtues Truth, "odor of a sublime life", and as a musical instrument used for "exultation of eternal

55 The fact that the children sit on the same axis as Job was first noticed by Delaney: The Iconography, p. 333.

56 Examples of illuminations for Job 1:20 are found in the following manuscripts: *749 Vaticanus gr.*, fol. 21, probably painted in Rome, in the second half of the 9th century; *Vaticanus gr. 1231*, probably painted in Cyprus in the early 12th century (both in Rome, Vatican Library); *Marciana gr. 538*, painted around 905 (Venice, Biblioteca Marciana); and in *Codex Gr. 5 (T)* (Greek Patriarchate, Jerusalem).

57 Verdier: L'allegoria della Misericordia, pp. 102–103.

58 Delaney: The Iconography, pp. 333–334.

praise".[59] He also adds, "the whole human race, which is chosen by the kindness of its Creator, and by the mercy of the same Redeemer, is designated by these names".[60]

The verse "and their father gave them inheritance among their brethren" (Job, 42:15) is explained by St. Gregory in the following manner: Christ (prefigured by Job) "admits the weak and humble to the lot of the heavenly inheritance",[61] meaning that within a Christian community, every person, including the weak, is accepted.

There are also visual aspects which link the *Sacred Allegory* to the traditional iconography of Job's daughters: as mentioned above, Bellini's painting features a woman wearing a crown, and there are also illustrations of the *Book of Job* depicting the daughters of both his first and second family as wearing crowns.[62]

There is also an illustration of the verse which describes the naming of Job's daughters, in which a figure appears to hold a horn above the head of one of his daughters.[63] Stella Papadaki-Oekland suggests that this illustration might refer to the name given to Job's third daughter, 'Keren Hapuch' (a kind of ancient eyes makeup, translated into English as 'the horn of adornment'), translated into Greek as 'Amalthea's Horn', the cornucopia of the goat that breastfed Zeus.[64] In the present context, it should be noted that in Bellini's painting, the canopy above the Virgin's head is resting on a cornucopia.

It is also worth noting that all of the manuscripts which describe Job's daughters as wearing crowns – as well as the manuscript including the cornucopia illustration described above – were found in Italy. Here, Bellini's interest in and active investigation of Byzantine art,[65] as demonstrated in his *San Giobbe Altarpiece*, are also worthy of mention, and thus, it is quite plausible that Bellini

59 St. Gregorius: *Moralia*, book XXXV, xvii, pp. 43–44. See also Delaney: The Iconography, p. 334.

60 St. Gregorius: *Moralia*, book XXXV, xvii, p. 43.

61 Ibid., book XXXV, xix, p. 46.

62 Illustrations are found in the following manuscripts (mentioned in fn. 48): an illustration of *Book of Job* 1:2 (first family) in *Marc. Gr. 538*, fol. 5v; illustrations of *Book of Job* 42:13–14 (second family) are found in *Vat. Gr.* 749, fol. 249v, and in a Coptic Bible manuscript of the 7th century, fol. 4v (National Library, Naples), *Naples IB 18*.

63 *Vaticanus gr. 751*, late12th to early 13th century, Vatican Library.

64 Papadaki-Oekland: *Illuminated Manuscripts*, pp. 169–170. See also Annette Yoshiko Reed: Job as Jobab, p. 34, fn. 10.

65 Joan Olivia Richardson: *Hodegetria and Venetia Virgo: Giovanni Bellini's San Giobbe Altarpiece*. MA thesis, University of British Columbia, 1979. https://circle.ubc.ca/handle/2429/21663 (accessed 17.06.2012), p. 74.

had contact with these manuscripts. Thus, while the interpretation of the figure on the throne as the Virgin Mary is undeniably the most plausible, it is possible that the three women depicted in the *Sacred Allegory* might also serve as subtle references to the three daughters of Job.

Now, let us return to the interpretation of the 'hovering' figure as St. Mary Magdalene: In the New Testament, St. Mary Magdalene is depicted as a sinner, excluded from society and reproached by the Apostles. Christ, however, forgives her, and indeed finds points in favor of her behavior.[66]

Here, we find a characteristic shared by St. Mary Magdalene and St. Paul: that of their penitence, which conferred upon them their saintly importance. Samuel Terrien maintains that the presence of St. Mary Magdalene and St. Sebastian in the *Sacred Allegory* is a reference to other outcasts or marginal people: and more specifically, those criminals convicted for sexual transgressions (St. Sebastian as the patron saint of homosexuals and St. Mary Magdalene as the patron saint of prostitutes). [67]

Taken together, these references appear to underscore the interpretation by St. Gregory quoted above, that there exists a place for everyone within the Christian community. More specifically, they appear to refer to the characteristics of inclusivity and compassion embedded in the structure of the Venetian community of this period.

Finally, there are two additional visual elements, which appear to support the hypothesis that the *Sacred Allegory* reflects Venetian society. The first is the colored marble floor of the terrace upon which the scene is set, which brings to mind the flooring typical of Venetian churches.[68] The second is the canopy above the Virgin's head, which can be read as an allusion to the canopy of the Doge of Venice.[69]

Conclusion

This paper demonstrates that the 15th century Venetians saw the Biblical figure of Job – as well as other saints – as pertinent to their social conditions. Job could represent various groups in the Venetian society of the late 15th to early 16th century, including the wealthy, the 'ashamed poor' and the 'worthy

66 Mark, 14:6; Luke, 7:35–50.

67 Terrien: *The Iconography of Job*, pp. 127–135.

68 Delaney: The Iconography, p. 335.

69 Richardson: *Hodegetria*, pp. 20, 117; Rona Goffen: *Piety and Patronage in Renaissance Venice: Bellini, Titian and the Franciscans.* New Haven: Yale UP 1986, pp. 156–157; Bätschmann: *Giovanni Bellini*, p. 138.

poor', who have always been integral to the fabric of Venetian society, and additionally the marginal, excluded poor, a group to which the Venetian *scuole* only began to provide assistance from the end of the 15th century. In turn, each of these groups could identify with the figure of Job.

The figures of the other saints featured in the picture corroborate these meanings, thus strengthening the connection between religious beliefs and social issues. This community of saints, portrayed in the painting, and to whom the faithful addressed their prayers, could reflect a Christian community characterized by solidarity and care for the poor, and especially the Venetian community with its special *scuole* structures. Furthermore, the fact that most of the saints are depicted in a prayer gesture and address their own prayers towards Christ the Child renders them as intercessors on behalf of this community.

Therefore, the painting also implies a kind of promise, since Job carried with him an optimistic message – not only because his social and economic status is restored at the end of the *Book of Job*. This promise has a double – and therefore an enhanced – meaning: first, on the religious level, one can read the painting as a group of mediating saints attentive to prayers and assisting people in need, and secondly, as shown in this article, on the social level, as a description of the Venetian society, which cares of all the poor and needy. And, thus, religion and social conditions are intertwined with each other in this enigmatic and fascinating painting.

Reviews

Malcolm McIntosh: *Japan Re-Armed.* London: Bloomsbury 2012.
Zachary S. Kopin

Following World War II, Japan underwent a radical reassessment of its role in the world. After close to a century of pursuing a policy of classical imperial expansion and contraction, the Japanese people ratified a document which fundamentally changed the way their state would operate in the post-war world. Written in the wake of the more than a decade of warfare that led up to the Japanese defeat, the Japanese Peace Constitution, and most notably Article 9, was an attempt to limit the power of the Japanese state from ever again causing another war. Article 9 states that the Japanese people "aspiring sincerely for an international peace [...] forever renounce war as a sovereign right of the nation" and that, in order to guarantee this, "land, sea and air forces, as well as other war potential, will never be maintained" by Japan. In *Japan Re-armed*, Malcolm McIntosh argues that a combination of economic growth, external threats and the passage of time are leading the Japanese government towards rejection of Article 9 of the Constitution of Japan.

McIntosh originally wrote this book in the mid-1980s, long before the collapse of the Soviet Union, Japan's lost decade, or the social, technological and economic change that the 21st century brought to the region. The text is exceedingly outdated. Bloomsbury's decision to produce a straight facsimile of the original 1986 text, going so far as to include the original cover page and publication information, limits its use to the modern reader. While Japan is still a nation with partners who are "to be traded with rather than aggressed," (p. 125) the threat of a Soviet Invasion of Hokkaido, which is a major issue in the text, is no longer relevant and Deng Xiaoping and Emperor Hirohito, both of whom appear as current, active actors in the work, are long dead. Had either the author or editor added even one page of para-textual material, it would have improved the relevancy of the text immensely. This book would best be used as a primary source, rather than a contemporary secondary one, in understanding the Japanese role in International Relations during the middle of the 1980s.

Although the text's frequent references to the Soviet Union are obviously outdated, China has replaced the Soviets as the biggest threat to Japanese security in the region, politically Japan has not changed a lot since McIntosh wrote the text. While the country is more nuclearly latent than it was in 1986 and Japan is considered by most to be only a turnkey away from a nuclear weapon, the current Prime Minister Shinzō Abe has done little to distance himself from his predecessors. Abe has publically visited the Yasukuni Shrine, something that McIntosh notes, with great dismay, Nakasone doing. The Shrine holds the remains of Japanese war dead, including those from World War II. Like Nakasone, Abe is a member of a right that wants to see a "rich country strongly armed" (p. 137). As McIntosh indicates, the greatest threat to Japanese security lies in economic, not military, weakness.

In a world in which America is pivoting her forces to East Asia, this book, however, still has a relevant purpose. After all, in such a situation, Nakasone's strategy of Japan being "one big aircraft carrier" (p. 117) would be central to American defense plans in the region. Ultimately, McIntosh's belief that "Japan could, through a non-offensive security outlook," which would maintain the spirit of Article 9, "positioned as she is with proximity to both China and the Soviet Union, and as one of the dynamos of the Pacific influence peace, security and stability in the 21st century," (p. 126) is as relevant today as it was then.

Rolf-Dieter Müller: *The Unknown Eastern Front: The Wehrmacht and Hitler's Foreign Soldiers.* London / New York: I. B. Tauris 2014.
James Horncastle

Recently, Second World War historiography has witnessed a critical re-evaluation of long held assumptions about the field. In particular, the issue of non-Germanic people's collaboration with Nazi Germany, which had previously been described strictly in visceral terms, has received increasing revisionist attention. The impact that collaboration had upon most societies has resulted in little analysis being done on the motivations and reasons behind their actions. Rolf-Dieter Müller's *The Unknown Eastern Front: The Wehrmacht and Hitler's Foreign Soldiers* attempts to examine what factors motivated individuals and countries to fight alongside and amongst the *Wehrmacht* on the Eastern Front. In so doing, Müller argues that the reasons and motivations for collaboration were diverse, and thus should not be regarded in Manichean terms, but rather in a much more nuanced form.

After introductory remarks, *The Unknown Eastern Front* is broken down into three sections: allies, volunteers from neutral and occupied territories, and Eastern European nations struggling against Stalinism. In the section on allies, Müller examines the varied reasons that led allied nations to support Germany on the Eastern Front. These ranged from Finland's pursuit of a parallel war to Italy's pursuit of territorial enlargement and keeping pace with its larger Axis ally (pp. 5–20, 68–88). In the section on neutral and occupied territories, Müller examines the motivations of soldiers from either occupied or sympathetic territories. Specifically, he examines the shared ideology that many of these groups had with Nazi Germany (pp. 107–108). Finally, in the section on Eastern European nations' struggle against Stalinism, Müller examines what motivated Eastern European nations to fight alongside the German Army, and how Nazi Germany, in particular Hitler, let racial ideology trump military expediency. This was, according to Müller, a fatal flaw in Germany's policy on the Eastern Front, particularly in regards to the Russians and Ukrainians (pp. 155–157). In some concluding remarks, Müller contends that historiography must take all of this into consideration and continue to push past the dichotomy between collaboration and resistance during Second World War by adding nuance to the issue.

While generally the argument of the book is strong, a number of issues detract from its persuasiveness. First, the author did not conduct research in many of the countries that he examines; therefore, the results are based largely on secondary literature. As a result, many of Müller's conclusions must be regarded as tentative, rather than conclusive. Second, because Müller is not an expert on these countries, key works, such as Jozo Tomasevich's *War and Revolution in Yugoslavia, 1941–1945: Occupation and Collaboration*[1], are not considered. Third, the manner in which quotes and firsthand accounts are incorporated is problematic. Rather than helping to build the overall argument, the quotes are not integrated in an effective manner. For example, Müller's incorporation of a Wehrmacht report to describe the actions of Latvian volunteers, while insightful, does not align with the previous point that he makes concerning German conscription efforts (p. 175). Thus, while firsthand accounts could have greatly aided the argument, they are instead relegated to the secondary purpose of lending color to the overall narrative.

Overall, the book provides a good foundation and introduction to readers who are unaware of the contribution that other nationalities had in the German army during the Second World War. That said, given the recent developments concerning the study of collaboration in the Second World War, the book is by no means revolutionary. Furthermore, rather taking a narrative approach to each nationality, the book would have benefitted from greater emphasis on analyzing the motives and reasons for collaboration, which come to the forefront in the conclusion. That being said, Müller's comprehensive examination of a variety of countries and nationalities provides a solid foundation for additional study.

Dhirendra K. Vajpeyi / Glen Segell (eds): *Civil-Military Relations in Developing Countries*. Lanham, MD: Lexington 2014.

Nathan Packard

During the period of decolonization that followed World War II, two institutions – the civilian bureaucracy and the local army – dominated political processes in newly independent countries. Time and again, aspiring political leaders turned to the military to assist in governance. As a result, the military assumed an overly influential role in policymaking. Although civilian control was held up as the ideal state of affairs, throughout the developing world the military as an institution emerged as a powerful political actor in its own right. This civil-military imbalance hindered representative governance in a number of developing countries as evidenced by the prevalence of military dictatorships.

1 Jozo Tomasevich: *War and Revolution in Yugoslavia, 1941–1945: Occupation and Collaboration.* Stanford: Stanford UP 2001.

Civil-Military Relations in Developing Countries, edited by Dhirendra Vajpeyi and Glen Segell, is a collection of essays on recent civil-military developments in countries in Africa, Asia, Latin America, and the Middle East. Much of the existing scholarship on civil-military relations addresses the United States and the Soviet Union during the Cold War or is otherwise Western-centric. On the other hand, civil-military relations in developing countries have been understudied in general; a trend that has become even more pronounced since the end of the Cold War. Thus, this book offers a much needed corrective.

The anthology begins with an introduction by the editors which discusses and critiques current models and literature on civil-military relations. The next seven chapters explore civil-military relations throughout the developing world. The main strength of the work is its broad scope. The countries covered include Botswana, China, El Salvador, Honduras, Guatemala, India, Indonesia, Nicaragua, Nigeria, Pakistan, Bahrain, Sudan, Iraq, Jordan, Saudi Arabia, Egypt, Tunisia, Yemen and Libya. Leading experts offer analyses on powerful countries, China and India for example, as well as smaller countries, such as Botswana, which have largely been neglected by scholars. In the process, the book accomplishes its goal of highlighting the diverse nature of civil-military relations in the developing world.

A second strength of the collection is that it captures the complexity of the civil-military relationship in the countries covered. According to Vajpeyi and Segell:

Civil-military relations in developing countries are no different from a coin, which has two inseparable sides. One side of the coin is the nature of civil-military relations with the development of the state associated with its evolving and developing political and economic systems. The other side of the coin is the role of the military in development including enacting peace and stability [...] thus the agency of soldiers is not only defense and deterrence but also development. (p. 1)

The case studies emphasize that the role of the military as an institution is not clear-cut. In some instances, militaries not only protected the state from external aggression but also played a positive role in economic development. In most countries, the military is one of the few institutions with the organizational and logistical capacity to act on a national scale. On the other hand, militaries have been used to violently suppress internal dissent and sustain unpopular regimes. Furthermore, corrupt military institutions and excessive defense expenditures can be a drain on the economy. According to the editors, the military has an important role to play; however, security sector reform is needed throughout the developing world to ensure that militaries do not interfere in governance. The central question for policymakers is how to create a military powerful enough to accomplish assigned missions without it becoming so formidable that it exerts undue influence in the economic and political spheres.

In the final analysis, *Civil-Military Relationships in Developing Countries* makes an important contribution to our understanding of the oversized role the military has played in the political life of developing countries. It will be of value to political scientists, students of international relations, as well as government and military professionals.

Table of Figures

Global Humanities
Studies in Histories, Cultures, and Societies

Edited by Frank Jacob

Published
01/2015 – On the Correlation of Center and Periphery
02/2015 – Religion and Poverty

Planned
03/2016 – Migration and State Power
04/2016 – Stereotypes and Violence
05/2017 – Gender and Public Opinion

Further information:
www.neofelis-verlag.de/zeitschriften-reihen/global-humanities/